Randi Whitney's Library
Enjoy all the books across multiple ger

Children's Books

Buffalo Nickel Ranch	Leaving Tracks
Who Let the Goat Out	The Blue Egg
I Love Buggy Rides	The Class with Heart
The Messes We Make	Leave Something Take Something
The Annual Cookie Tree	Tomato Boy
It's Valentines, of Course of Course	Every Letter Counts
The Community Can	Chocolate Chip Cookies
Be Three	Louis, Louis

Young Children's Chapter Books

The Ranch Coin	The Cookie Tree Tradition
Buggy Rides	The Biggest Mess
The Great Goatsby	The Green Egg
The Community Colection	The Lost Medal

Early Reader Picture Books

The Other Side of the Nickel   The Goat's Gate

Educational Books

Reading for Retrieval	4 Dimensions of Comprehension
Writing for Purpose	Grammatical Matters
Teach BIG: Believe in Greatness – Bring Best Practices Back	Lexicon Mysteries Solved
	Fluency Flows
Teach BIG: Believe in Greatness – Study Guide	GAP Phonics: Preventing and Closing Gaps

Mystery/Thriller Novels

A Good Witness   The Knock   The Teacher Retreat   Twisted Poison

Christian Novels

The Last Day   The First Day

Motivational Books

Don't Spend Your CAN Years CAN'Ting

Preteen Christian Chapter Books

The Bookcase: Matthew	The Bookcase: John
The Bookcase: Mark	The Bookcase: Acts
The Bookcase: Luke	The Bookcase: Romans

SCAN ME!

randiwhitney.com
teachbig.com

Teach BIG Portfolio

(Home of The Writing Academy)

3502 Columbia Memorial Parkway, Kemah, TX 77565. 281-549-4466

teachbig.com

Randi Whitney, founder of Teach Big/The Writing Academy, has been the keynote and motivational speaker for over 25 years at numerous conventions and seminars where she has gained critical acclaim from teachers and administrators alike. Having been a classroom teacher and current owner of a teacher training facility and an early childhood preparatory school, Mrs. Whitney takes great pride in encouraging teachers to find joy in children through her Teach BIG approach. Her special gift of communication is evident as the audience laughs out loud and is brought to sentimental tears. Mrs. Whitney's message takes the audience back to their childhoods and reminds them of what a difference a teacher can make!

Teach BIG Abstract Overview
Teach BIG is a comprehensive instructional framework that equips educators to deliver high-impact language arts instruction through clarity, consistency, and content mastery. Rooted in research and real classroom practice, Teach BIG offers tools and training across six essential areas: phonics, grammar, vocabulary, fluency, comprehension, and constructed response writing. With its signature systems—like the Full Circle of Language Arts, the Four Dimensions of Comprehension, and daily flipbooks—Teach BIG helps teachers become confident content experts who close gaps and grow readers and writers. Whether used in public schools, private settings, or homeschool environments, Teach BIG transforms instruction into a purposeful and empowering experience for both teachers and students.

Mission Statement: Teach BIG equips teachers to become experts in content, craft and complements so that cognition and confidence soar for all people.

Catalog Delivered Upon Request: Teach BIG Catalog ISBN number is: 978-1-966301-47-9

What is Teach BIG/The Writing Academy?
Teach BIG is a comprehensive, research-based instructional framework and professional development system that equips educators to become confident, content-rich experts in **language arts instruction**. It stands for more than a teaching method—it's a philosophy rooted in the belief that when teachers are empowered with deep knowledge and daily habits, students thrive in reading, writing, speaking, and listening.

At its heart, **Teach BIG** is about **clarity, consistency, and content mastery**. It provides the tools, training, and instructional materials needed for teachers to deliver high-impact instruction across six core areas:

1. Phonics
2. Grammar
3. Vocabulary
4. Fluency
5. Reading Comprehension
6. Written Constructed Response

These six areas form the **Full Circle of Language Arts**, a structured framework that connects each literacy skill to ensure student success.

Teach BIG offers:

- Professional development for teachers and leaders
- TEKS-aligned training and instructional materials
- Daily-use classroom flipbooks and anchor tools
- A robust online platform with assessments and digital support
- Podcasts, children's books, intervention tools, and real-time teacher advice systems

Teach BIG is used in public schools, private schools, and homeschool settings. It also includes campus certification models like **LEAP Schools**, leadership retreats at **Buffalo Nickel Ranch**, and teacher content books like *Reading for Retrieval, Grammar School, Phonics Forever, Lexicon Mysteries Solved*, and many more.

Ultimately, Teach BIG transforms classroom instruction by building **teacher expertise**, aligning to **state standards**, and creating **students who believe in their own greatness**.

If you're an educator who wants to teach with passion, precision, and power—**Teach BIG** is for you.

Endorsements/Credentials/Committees:
TEA Instructional Materials Certification as listed on the TEA Website:
- ERLA K-5 IM Select the full-subject and/or supplemental publisher(s)/product(s) that teachers in your LEA will use regularly (once a week or more, on average) for English RLA grades K–2 instruction to ensure coverage of 100% of the TEKS. (page 5)
- Q5.1 Select the full-subject and/or supplemental publisher(s)/product(s) that teachers in your LEA will use regularly (once a week or more, on average) for English RLA grades 3–5 instruction to ensure coverage of 100% of the TEKS (page 11)
- Q6.1 Select full-subject and/or supplemental publisher(s)/product(s) that teachers in your LEA will regularly use (once a week or more, on average) for Spanish RLA grades K–2 instruction to ensure coverage of 100% of the TEKS (do not include products used to build classroom libraries). (page 17)
- Q6.2 Select full-subject and/or supplemental publisher(s)/product(s) that teachers in your LEA will regularly use (once a week or more, on average) for Spanish RLA grades 3–5 instruction to ensure coverage of 100% of the TEKS (do not include products used to build classroom libraries). (page 22)

WBEA Certification 2016 to present - WBENC National Certification Number: 2005129107
HUB Certificate VID Number 1811756460100Early Childhood Endorsement from the University of Houston at Clear Lake
TCC Board Member at UHCL
CDA Credentials from the State of Texas (Operation Number 1064587)
Good Reads Author

Professional Publications/Accomplishments:
Holds Multiple Registered Trademarks (#2,780,923)
Holds over 100 ISBNs for educational works, children's books, and novels
Published Author of 20 Children's Books (Amazon.com) in English and Spanish
Published Author of 4 Chapter Books (Amazon.com)
Published Author of 4 T-TESS Training Manuals (Amazon.com)
Published Author of 2 Novels (Amazon.com)
Published Author of 1 Self-Help Inspirational Book *Don't Spend Your CAN Years CAN'Ting* (Amazon.com)
Published Author of over 100 Teacher Training Manuals and Curriculum Guides
Author of the Motivational Book, Teach BIG! (ISBN #978-1-4675-9178-2)
Owner of Multiple Websites: teachbig.com, strawberryprep.org, randiwhitney.com
Owner of 430-acre Teacher Training Facility (buffalonickelranch.com)
Publication in the Professional Education Journal "Educational Leadership"

Speaking Experience:
Conducted Lunch-n-Learn Webinars for TEPSA (Texas Elementary Principals and Supervisors Association)
Keynote and Breakout Speaker at Multiple Professional Conferences:
    TEPSA (Texas Elementary Principals and Supervisors Association) 26 years consecutively
        Region 4 TEPSA

HISD – 4th Grade Writing Summit (Keynote Speaker) – multiple years
AEA Conference (Arizona Education Association Conference)
KASSP (Kentucky Association Secondary School Principals)
MAESP (Missouri Association Education School Principals)
ASCD (Association of Supervision and Curriculum Development)
ADE (Arkansas Department of Education)
FASA (Florida Association of School Administrators)
NAPHS (National Association of Private & Home Schools)
NAEYC (National Association for the Education of Young Children)
NYSEC (New York State Education Conference)
PSEA (Pennsylvania State Education Association)
TPA (Tennessee Principal's Association)
TASA (Texas Association of School Administrators)
GHSA (Great Homeschool Association)
TLA (Texas Librarian Association)
TXTELA (Texas Teachers of English Language Arts)
TEKSCON (TEKS Conference)
All ESCs over the course of many years

Types of Specialized Training:

- Specialized teacher content trainings
- Student CAMP trainings in English and Spanish
- Student classroom lessons in English and Spanish
- WAVE virtual teacher training factor
- Virtual student trainings
- SLIFE trainings
- Teacher make and take trainings
- SHAPE Leadership/Administrative Training
- T-TESS/TIA Professional Development Trainings

Online Practice Assessment Platform: Teach BIG OnSTAGE
The Teach BIG OnStage Online Assessment Platform is a comprehensive, TEKS-aligned digital resource designed to enhance language arts instruction for students in grades 2–10 in English and Spanish. It offers monthly practice passages across subjects like science, social studies, and fine arts, featuring STAAR 2.0-style questions and interactive tools such as highlighting, text-to-speech, and note-taking. Teachers benefit from automatic grading, detailed TEKS correlations, and customizable reports, facilitating data-driven instruction and targeted interventions. With three subscription levels—Assessments, Bridge, and Curriculum—educators can access a range of resources, including instructional videos, printable materials, and daily lesson plans, all aimed at building student confidence and mastery in language arts.

TEKS Specialized Materials: (all materials are based on the Texas TEKS. This specialized line in designed to teach the individual distinctions between each word, including the Breakout terminology (including, and, or, such), the effects that the parts of speech have on the TEKS in specific, and the difference between content and skills. The Teach BIG TEKS Training is inherently the optimum starting point and basis for all Language arts training regardless of curriculum utilized.

- In-Depth Study of the TEKS Teacher Training Manual and Workbook
- ELAR TEKS Lesson Plans for Breakout TEKS (Standard 1)
- ELAR TEKS Lesson Plans for Breakout TEKS (Standard 2A)
- ELAR TEKS Lesson Plans for Breakout TEKS (Standard 2B-C)
- ELAR TEKS Lesson Plans for Breakout TEKS (Standards 3-5)
- ELAR TEKS Lesson Plans for Breakout TEKS (Standard 6)
- ELAR TEKS Lesson Plans for Breakout TEKS (Standards 7-8)
- ELAR TEKS Lesson Plans for Breakout TEKS (Standard 9)
- ELAR TEKS Lesson Plans for Breakout TEKS (Standard 10)
- ELAR TEKS Lesson Plans for Breakout TEKS (Standard 11 A-C)
- ELAR TEKS Lesson Plans for Breakout TEKS (Standard 11 D-E)
- ELAR TEKS Lesson Plans for Breakout TEKS (Standards 12-13)

Catalog Overview: Catalog ISBN #978-1-966301-37-0

- A **full suite of professional content training manuals** that provide teachers with the **background knowledge** needed to become high-fidelity language arts instructors. Titles include: Phonics *Forever, Grammar School, Lexicon Mysteries Solved, Fluency Fundamentals, Reading for Retrieval,* and *Writing with Purpose.* With excellent curriculum in place, administrators often find that the missing link is the level of true language arts content understanding. Teach BIG fills the knowledge gap for educators!
- **TEKS Deep-Dive Trainings** designed to help teachers break down the standards in a way they've never experienced. After undergoing the rigorous process of getting Teach BIG materials listed on the **Texas Education Agency's Instructional Materials Certification list**, I developed a publisher-level understanding of the TEKS. I now offer training that guides educators through that same deep, structural approach—revealing the powerful instructional clarity often missed in surface-level planning.
- The **Full Circle of Language Arts Literacy** framework—covering phonics, grammar, vocabulary, fluency, comprehension, and constructed response—with an **eight-month "Closing the Gap" flipbook for each literacy habit**, designed to serve as an effective intervention tool for struggling learners that compliments a district's current curriculum
- An **online assessment platform** that mimics the **STAAR test format button-for-button**, including **short constructed response (SCR)** and **extended constructed response (ECR)** blocks with live **character-count response tools**, helping students develop test-aligned writing fluency and confidence.
- The **Get in SHAPE Teacher Training Series**, which supports **professional growth through the T-TESS lens**, aligned to each of the four T-TESS domains. The titles include: *The Full*

Circle of Teaching, Beyond the Script, Posters to Passion, and *The Diamond Teacher.* This series of books and trainings is designed to help teachers achieve their desired observation results and reach their TIA goals.
- A growing catalog of **children and student books** that serve as high-interest, literacy-aligned mentor texts, including content books for students like *Decode Mode, The Day the Sentences Stormed In* and *The Thread,* children's books including *Who Let the Goat Out?, Buggy Rides, Buffalo Nickel Ranch,* and *The Messes We Make,* and chapter books for young readers like *The Great Goatsby, The Ranch Coin,* and *The Cookie Tree.*
- A **podcast**—*Teach BIG*—that features practical insights and **guest educators who embody our Believe in Greatness philosophy.** Available on Spotify, Apple Podcasts, iHeartRadio, and the Teach BIG website.
- A **professional training center** in Crockett, Texas, situated on 430 acres, featuring a 70-person conference facility, gourmet meals, and overnight lodging for up to 60 guests—**where we would love to offer a leadership training for your leadership team!**
- National presentations at **state and regional conferences**, teacher retreats, and literacy summits, along with **Virtual WAVE Lessons**, where I join classrooms virtually to team-teach and model instructional delivery in real time

Instructional Frameworks/System:

- **Full Circle of Language Arts (FCLA)** – Six interconnected teacher training manuals addressing the 6 areas of literacy: Phonics, Grammar, Vocabulary, Fluency, Reading Comprehension, and Written Constructed Response
- **Four Dimensions of Comprehension** – Taught, Tap, Think, Toggle (levels of thinking required to answer questions)
- **RAP Fluency System** – Rate, Accuracy, Prosody leading to fluency
- **TRACKS Annotation System** – Evidence collection technique for close reading and test preparation
- **CSI Framework** – Connect to the prompt, Support the thesis, Infer additional ideas (written constructed response support for collecting relevant textual evidence)
- **GRADUATE Framework** – System/Steps for ensuring a complete and infinite lesson cycle

T-TESS and TIA Support:

- *Full Circle of Language Arts* (Domain 1)
- *Beyond the Script* (Domains 1,2)
- *Posters to Passions* (Domain 3)
- *The Diamond Teacher* (Domain 4)

Teach BIG Professional Training Center: The Teach BIG Teacher Training Center, situated at Buffalo Nickel Ranch in Crockett, Texas, offers educators a unique and immersive professional development experience. Spanning 430 acres, this serene environment is designed to foster learning, reflection, and collaboration among teachers. The center provides a variety of training programs, including the renowned Ranch Retreats, which combine high-energy, hands-on workshops with the tranquility of the ranch setting. Accommodations on-site allow participants to fully engage in the experience, promoting deeper connections and a focus on instructional growth. Located conveniently between Houston and Dallas, the Teach BIG Training Center serves as a hub for educators seeking to enhance their skills in language arts instruction and beyond.

Grant Writing Information: Please visit our website (teachbig.com) and click on the tab labeled Correlations to view all of the connections that teach big has with the TEKS, the STAAR test, various crosswalks, Alignment to amplify bluebonnet, alignment to HMH, alignment to SAVVAS, and many more alignments in the educational arena.

Media Exposure:

- Podcast – Teach BIG (available on all platforms and the Teach BIG website) – new episodes each Monday
- USA News Article (see website to read complete article featuring Teach BIG's *Beyond the Script* Book
- News Network appearances – See website to view the broadcasts
- TLC Network – 7 seasons on *OutDaughtered*

Social Media: Instagram (@teach_big), Facebook (@teach_big), Pinterest (@TeachBig3502), TikTok (@teachbig), YouTube (@Teach-Big)

PODCAST DETAILS

Title of Podcast: Teach BIG

Host: Randi Whitney

Podcast Location: Spotify, Apple Podcast, iHeart Radio, YouTube, our website

Niche: Public/Private/Homeschool Educators, Administrators, Interventionists

Frequency: Each Monday

Website: teachbig.com

Growing authentic teachers in an automated world

THANK YOU!

Follow Us on Social Media

@teach_big   @teach_big   @TeachBig3502   @teachbig   @Teach-Big

TEACH BIG CATALOG

Teach Big!
3502 Columbia Memorial Pkwy
Kemah, TX 77565

Phone: (281) 549-4466
Email: welcome@teachbig.com
Website: teachbig.com

ACTIVITY BOOKS

	Full Circle Collection | 4th Grade Social Studies **SKU:** 8098	$20.00
	Spelling Spirals | This resource is great for grades 3-8. **SKU:** 3067	$12.00
	Sentence Weather | This resource is great for grades 3-8. **SKU:** 3066	$12.00
	I Spy Fry Phrases **SKU:** 9049	$12.00
	Mastering Morphemes **SKU:** 9048	$12.00
	Phonics Diagnostic Tool **SKU:** 9019	$20.00

	How to Run a Restaurant SKU: 9017	$12.00
	Full Circle Collection | 5th Grade Social Studies SKU: 9007	$20.00
	Sound Blocks SKU: 9005	$12.00
	Full Circle Collection | 5th Grade Science SKU: 9001	$20.00
	Full Circle Collection | 3rd Grade Social Studies SKU: 8095	$20.00
	The Gen-Rule Battle | High Frequency Words SKU: 8088	$12.00
	Arguing with Purpose | This resource is great for grades 6-12. SKU: 8078	$12.00
	Grammar Bricks - Science | This resource is great for grades 3-8 SKU: 8072	$12.00
	3-8 Science Lexicon Mysteries SKU: 8070	$12.00
	Elaboration Station | This resource is great for grades 3-8. SKU: 3046	$12.00
	Everyday Writing | This resource is great for grades 3-8. SKU: 3000	$10.00

	Comma Drama	This resource is great for grades 3-8. **SKU:** 2091	$12.00
	Grammar Bricks - Misused and Confused **SKU:** 1133	$12.00
	How to Become an Athlete	This document has a total of 43 pages. **SKU:** 1103	$12.00
	Vocabulary Nation! **SKU:** 9047	$12.00
	That's Inspiring - Fluency Practice **SKU:** 9046	$12.00
	Collocations **SKU:** 9045	$12.00
	Research Briefs **SKU:** 9038	$12.00
	G.A.P Phonics Cumulative Flashcards	Sound Collections For: Vowels and Consonants **SKU:** 8083	$12.00
	Attention to Comprehension **SKU:** 9035	$12.00
	Paragraph Power K-2	Science & Social Studies **SKU:** 9024	$12.00
	Literary Analysis Grades 6-12 **SKU:** 9023	$12.00

	**Phoneme Booklets	A Collection of Booklets Addressing: Consonants & Vowels** SKU: 9022	$12.00
	How to Write a Research Paper SKU: 9021	$12.00
	How to Write a Novel SKU: 9020	$12.00
	Prosody Practice With High Frequency Words SKU: 9018	$12.00
	Prosody Practice Within Science & Social Studies SKU: 9016	$12.00
	**Selection Collection 3-5	Science** SKU: 9010	$12.00
	**Full Circle Collection	4th Grade Science** SKU: 8096	$20.00
	The 4 Dimensions of Comprehension & Response SKU: 8091	$12.00
	Direct Decodables Collection SKU: 8089	$100.00
	**The Gen-Rule Battle	Science and Social Studies** SKU: 8087	$12.00
	**G.A.P Phonics Cumulative Flashcards	Sound Collections For: Vowel Teams R-Controlled and Diphthongs** SKU: 8085	$12.00

 G.A.P. Phonics Cumulative Flashcards : Sound Collections for : Common Blends and Digraphs $12.00
SKU: 8079

 Misused and Confused | This resources is great for grades 6-8. $12.00
SKU: 8075

 Misused and Confused | This resources is great for grades 3-5. $12.00
SKU: 8074

 Paper Plate: Writing Power | This resource is great for grades 3-8. $12.00
SKU: 3065

 Miracle Moments $12.00
SKU: 1244

 Fables, Fairytales, and Fiction $12.00
SKU: 1243

 Fluency Flipbook: Small Group Lessons Making Big Differences, Level 2 $49.00
SKU: 1241

 Grammar Flipbook: Small Group Lessons Making Big Differences, Level 2 $49.00
SKU: 1135

 Phonics Flipbook: Small Group Lessons Making Big Differences, Level 2 $49.00
SKU: 1136

 The Very Good Book "Late" $8.00
SKU: 1102

 The Very Good Book "Early" $8.00
SKU: 1101

The Very Good Book "Light" (Heavy and Light) SKU: 1100		$8.00
The Very Good Book "Heavy" SKU: 9099		$8.00
The Very Good Book "Good" SKU: 9098		$8.00
The Very Good Book "Bad" SKU: 9097		$8.00
The Really Good Book "Thin" SKU: 9096		$8.00
The Very Good Book "Thick" SKU: 9095		$8.00
The Very Good Book "Weak" SKU: 9094		$8.00
The Very Good Book "Strong" SKU: 9093		$8.00
The Very Good Book "Front" SKU: 9092		$8.00
The Very Good Book "Back" SKU: 9091		$8.00
The Very Good Book "Sweet" SKU: 9090		$8.00

The Very Good Book "Sour" SKU: 9089		$8.00
The Very Good Book "Dirty" SKU: 9088		$8.00
The Very Good Book "Clean" SKU: 9087		$8.00
The Very Good Book "Wet" SKU: 9086		$8.00
The Very Good Book "Dry" SKU: 9085		$8.00
The Very Good Book "Right" SKU: 9084		$8.00
The Very Good Book "Left" SKU: 9083		$8.00
The Very Good Book "Near" SKU: 9082		$8.00
The Very Good Book "Far" SKU: 9081		$8.00
The Very Good Book "Tall" SKU: 9080		$8.00
The Very Good Book "Short" SKU: 9079		$8.00

	The Very Good Book "Quiet" SKU: 9078	$8.00
	The Very Good Book "Loud" SKU: 9077	$8.00
	The Very Good Book "Soft" SKU: 9076	$8.00
	The Very Good Book "Hard" SKU: 9075	$8.00
	The Very Good Book "Night" SKU: 9074	$8.00
	The Very Good Book "Day" SKU: 9073	$8.00
	The Very Good Book "Out" SKU: 9072	$8.00
	The Very Good Book "In" SKU: 9071	$8.00
	The Very Good Book "Up" SKU: 9070	$8.00
	The Very Good Book "Down" SKU: 9069	$8.00
	The Very Good Book "Full" SKU: 9068	$8.00

	The Very Good Book "Empty" SKU: 9067	$8.00
	The Very Good Book "Young" SKU: 9066	$8.00
	The Very Good Book "Old" SKU: 9065	$8.00
	The Very Good Book " Open" SKU: 9064	$8.00
	The Very Good Book "Closed" SKU: 9063	$8.00
	The Very Good Book "Light" (Dark and Light) SKU: 9062	$8.00
	The Very Good Book "Dark" SKU: 9061	$8.00
	The Very Good Book "Sad" SKU: 9060	$8.00
	The Very Good Book "Happy" SKU: 9059	$8.00
	The Very Good Book "Slow" SKU: 9058	$8.00
	The Very Good Book "Fast" SKU: 9057	$8.00

	The Very Good Book "Small" SKU: 9056	$8.00
	The Very Good Book "Big" SKU: 9055	$8.00
	The Very Good Book "Hot" SKU: 9054	$8.00
	The Very Good Book "Cold" SKU: 9053	$8.00
	TEKS Tribune Ancillary Book SKU: 9050	$12.00
	What Happened Next? SKU: 9044	$12.00
	Everyday Etymology Cards SKU: 9043	$12.00
	Fluency Flows SKU: 9042	$12.00
	Look It Up! SKU: 9041	$12.00
	Out of Sorts SKU: 9040	$12.00
	What Happens When? SKU: 9039	$12.00

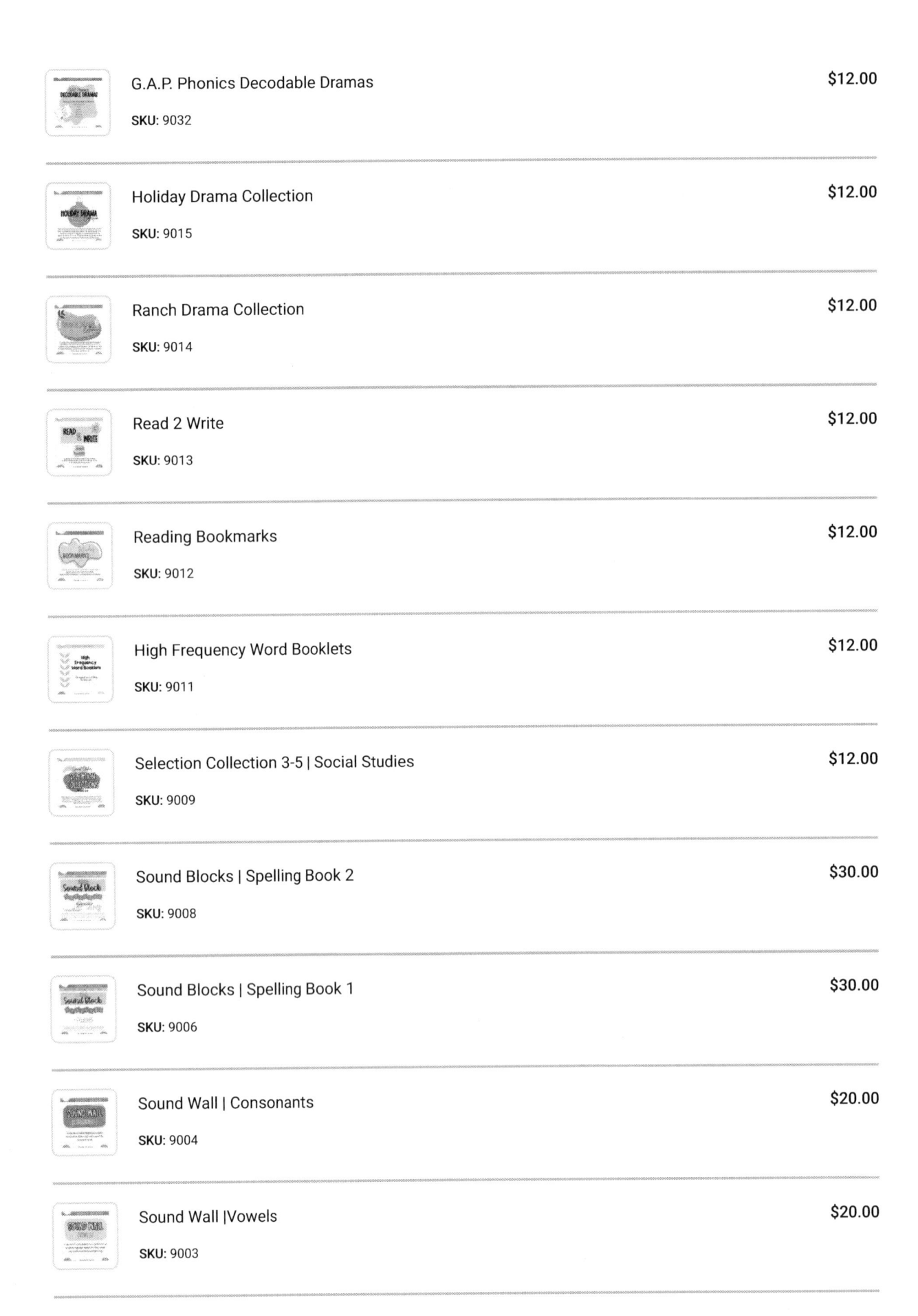

	G.A.P. Phonics Decodable Dramas SKU: 9032	$12.00
	Holiday Drama Collection SKU: 9015	$12.00
	Ranch Drama Collection SKU: 9014	$12.00
	Read 2 Write SKU: 9013	$12.00
	Reading Bookmarks SKU: 9012	$12.00
	High Frequency Word Booklets SKU: 9011	$12.00
	Selection Collection 3-5	Social Studies SKU: 9009	$12.00
	Sound Blocks	Spelling Book 2 SKU: 9008	$30.00
	Sound Blocks	Spelling Book 1 SKU: 9006	$30.00
	Sound Wall	Consonants SKU: 9004	$20.00
	Sound Wall |Vowels SKU: 9003	$20.00

	TEACH BIG Poster Set SKU: 9002	$30.00
	TEKS Specific Certificates 6-10 SKU: 9000	$12.00
	**TEKS Task Cards 6-7	Science** SKU: 8099	$12.00
	**TEKS Task Cards 6-7	Social Studies** SKU: 8097	$12.00
	**TEKS Task Cards 8-10	Science** SKU: 8094	$12.00
	**TEKS Task Cards 8-10	Social Studies** SKU: 8092	$12.00
	Flash Foldables SKU: 8090	$12.00
	Decodable Dramas SKU: 8086	$12.00
	Daily Decisions SKU: 8084	$12.00
	**Coloration Annotation - Social Studies	This resource is great for grades 3-5.** SKU: 8082	$12.00
	**Coloration Annotation - Science	This resource is great for grades 3-5.** SKU: 8081	$12.00

	Break It Up : A Drama About Breaking Words Into Syllables SKU: 8080	$12.00
	Alphabet Stick Figures Cumulative Flashcards SKU: 8077	$12.00
	Misused and Confused	This resources is great for grades 9-12 SKU: 8076	$12.00
	Grammar Bricks - Social Studies	This resource is great for grades 3-8 SKU: 8073	$12.00
	3-8 Social Studies Lexicon Mysteries SKU: 8071	$12.00
	Spelling Spirals	This resource is great for grades pk-2. SKU: 3071	$12.00
	Lexicon Mysteries: The Original Sleuth	This resource is great for grades pk-2. SKU: 3070	$12.00
	Jasper's Jambalaya	This resource is great for grades pk-2. SKU: 3069	$12.00

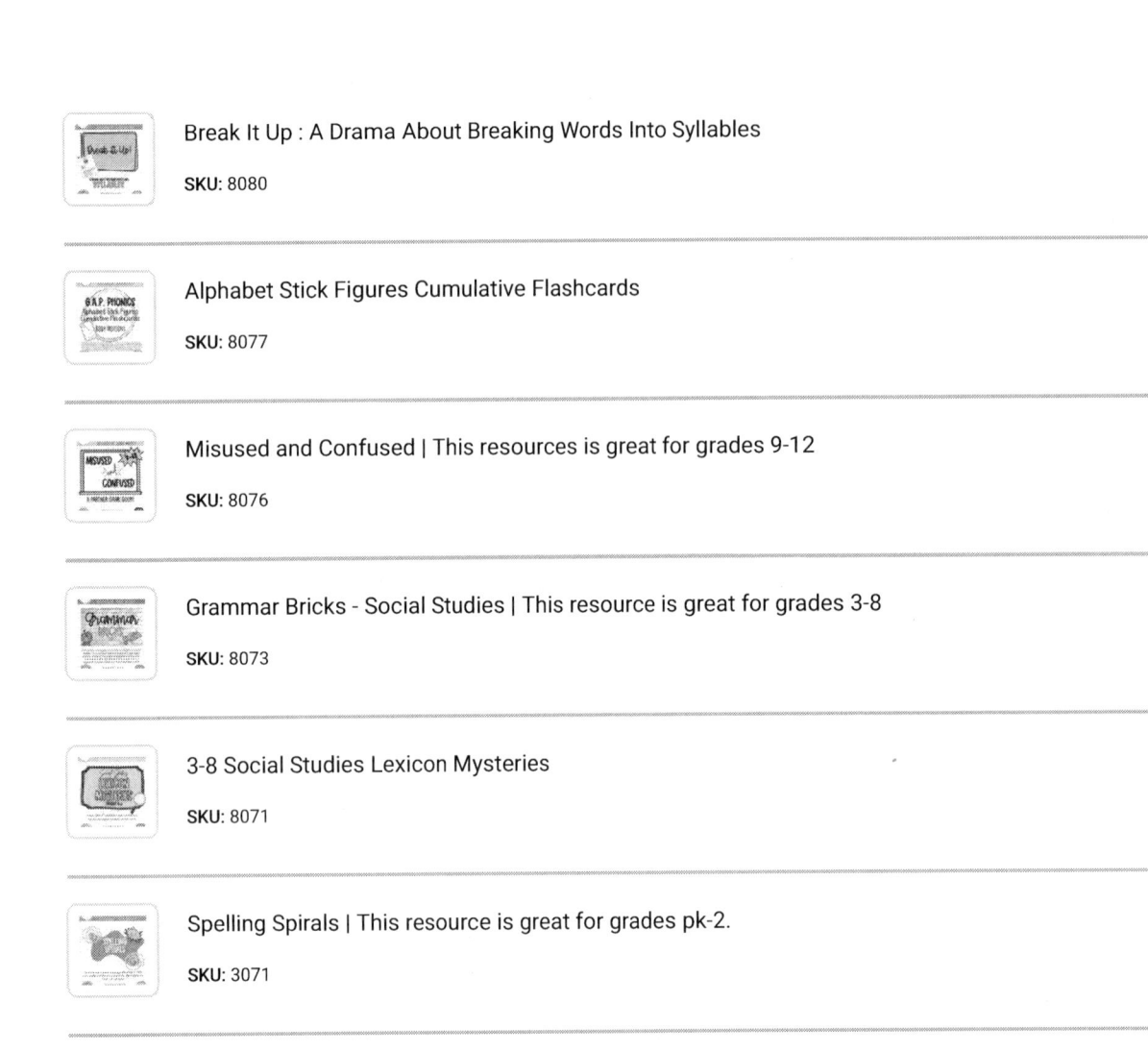

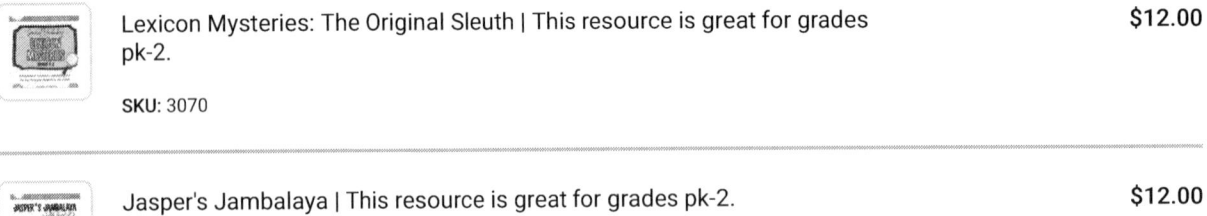

BOOKS

	Everyone Knows Fluency Flows: Fluency SKU: 1240	$11.99
	Goosebottom Gazette: Grammar SKU: 1239	$11.99
	Mailbox Mouse: Editing SKU: 1238	$11.99
	The Hidden Thread: Theme SKU: 1237	$11.99
	The Goat's Gate: An Easy Reader to Accompany Who Let the Goat Out? (Buffalo Nickel Ranch Children's Books) SKU: 1236	$8.99
	Rancho Buffalo Nickel (Buffalo Nickel Ranch Children's Books) (Spanish Edition) SKU: 1235	$12.99
	I Love Buggy Rides (Buffalo Nickel Ranch Children's Books) SKU: 1234	$12.99
	The Other Side of the Nickel: An Easy Reader Version of Buffalo Nickel Ranch (Buffalo Nickel Ranch Children's Books) SKU: 1233	$8.99
	Quien Dejo Salir a la Cabra (Buffalo Nickel Ranch Children's Books) (Spanish Edition) SKU: 1232	$12.99

	Me Encantan Los Paseos en el Carrito (Buffalo Nickel Ranch Children's Books) (Spanish Edition) SKU: 1231	$12.99
	Los Desastres que Hecemos (Buffalo Nickel Ranch Children's Books) (Spanish Edition) SKU: 1230	$12.99
	It's Valentine's Of Course, Of Course! SKU: 1229	$12.99
	El Huevo Azul (Buffalo Nickel Ranch Children's Books) (Spanish Edition) SKU: 1228	$12.99
	The Class With Heart (Buffalo Nickel Ranch Children's Books) SKU: 1227	$12.99
	The Annual Cookie Tree: A Christmas Tradition (Buffalo Nickel Ranch Children's Books) SKU: 1226	$9.99
	Teach BIG! Study Guide SKU: 1225	$11.99
	Buggy Rides: The Power of Bravery (Buffalo Nickel Ranch) SKU: 1224	$14.99
	The Cookie Tree: The Power of Tradition (Buffalo Nickel Ranch) SKU: 1223	$14.99
	The Great Goatsby: The Power of Responsibility (Buffalo Nickel Ranch) SKU: 1222	$14.99
	Every Letter Counts (Buffalo Nickel Ranch Children's Books) SKU: 1221	$12.99

	Leave Something, Take Something (Buffalo Nickel Ranch Children's Books) SKU: 1220	$12.99
	The Messes We Make (Buffalo Nickel Ranch Children's Books) SKU: 1219	$12.99
	The Blue Egg (Buffalo Nickel Ranch Children's Books) SKU: 1218	$12.99
	Don't Spend Your CAN Years CAN'Ting SKU: 1217	$11.99
	ELAR TEKS Lesson Plans - TEKS 2A (Teach BIG!) SKU: 1216	$14.99
	ELAR TEKS Lesson Plans - TEKS 2 B-C (Teach BIG!) SKU: 1215	$14.99
	ELAR TEKS Lesson Plans - TEKS 9 (Teach BIG!) SKU: 1214	$14.99
	Teach BIG!: Believe in Greatness - Bring Best Practices Back SKU: 1213	$19.99
	ELAR TEKS Lesson Plans - TEKS 12-13 (Teach BIG!) SKU: 1212	$14.99
	ELAR TEKS Lesson Plans - TEKS 1 (Teach BIG!) SKU: 1211	$14.99
	Tomato Boy (Buffalo Nickel Ranch Children's Books) SKU: 1210	$12.99

	ELAR TEKS Lesson Plans - TEKS 11 A-C (Teach BIG!) SKU: 1209	$14.99
	ELAR TEKS Lesson Plans - TEKS 11 D-E (Teach BIG!) SKU: 1208	$14.99
	ELAR TEKS Lesson Plans - TEKS 7-8 (Teach BIG!) SKU: 1207	$14.99
	ELAR TEKS Lesson Plans - TEKS 3-5 (Teach BIG!) SKU: 1206	$14.99
	A Good Witness SKU: 1205	$19.99
	Leaving Tracks (Buffalo Nickel Ranch Children's Books) SKU: 1204	$12.99
	ELAR TEKS Lesson Plans - TEKS 10 (Teach BIG!) SKU: 1203	$14.99
	ELAR TEKS Lesson Plans - TEKS 6 (Teach BIG!) SKU: 1202	$14.99
	The WRITE to Argue: A Comprehensive Guide to Teaching Argumentative Writing (Full Circle Series) SKU: 1201	$29.99
	Lexicon Mysteries Solved: How to Teach Vocabulary in Every Tier to Every Student (Full Circle Series) SKU: 1200	$29.99
	Fluency Fundamentals: Empowering Teachers to Build Confident, Expressive Readers (Full Circle Series) SKU: 1199	$29.99

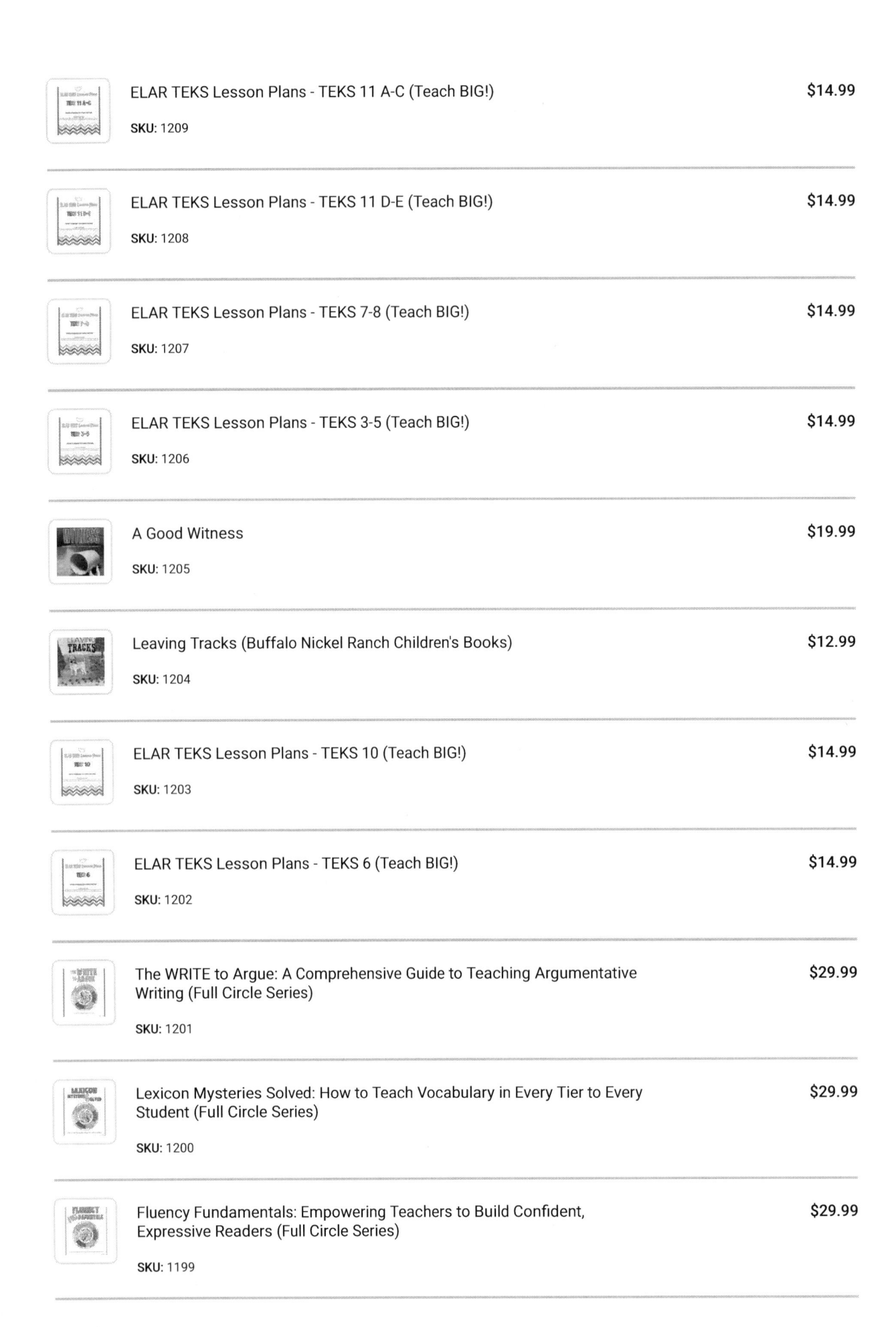

	Reading for Retrieval (Full Circle Series) SKU: 1198	$29.99
	Writing with Purpose: An In-depth Study into the 4 Dimensions of Comprehension & Written Constructed Response (Full Circle Series) SKU: 1197	$29.99
	Beyond the Script: Teacher Edition SKU: 1196	$14.99
	The Ranch Coin: The Power of Perspective (Buffalo Nickel Ranch) SKU: 1195	$14.99
	The Diamond Teacher (Teach BIG!) SKU: 1194	$9.99
	The Knock SKU: 1193	$13.99
	Full Circle of Language Arts: Where Content Meets Purpose and Gaps Meet Their End (Full Circle Series) SKU: 1192	$14.99
	Posters to Passion SKU: 1191	$14.99
	Phonics Forever (Full Circle Series) SKU: 1190	$29.99
	The Bookcase (Matthew): A Bible Journey through the Eyes of a Preteen (The Bookcase Series) SKU: 1189	$12.99
	Grammar School: BEST Practices in Editing and Revising for All Curriculum Types (Full Circle Series) SKU: 1188	$29.99

The Day the Sentences Stormed In (Full Circle Series) **SKU:** 1187		$11.99
An In-Depth Study of the Texas TEKS (Teach BIG!) **SKU:** 1186		$29.99
The Curious Case of the Clues (Teach BIG!) **SKU:** 1185		$11.99
Buffalo Nickel Ranch (Buffalo Nickel Ranch Children's Books) **SKU:** 1184		$12.99
Who Let the Goat Out? (Buffalo Nickel Ranch Children's Book) **SKU:** 1183		$12.99

BUFFALO NICKEL RANCH DRAMAS / POETRY

A Drama Experience | Buffalo Nickel Ranch — $15.00
SKU: 4091

A Drama Experience | I Love Buggy Rides — $15.00
SKU: 4059

A Drama Experience | Leaving Tracks — $15.00
SKU: 5000

A Drama Experience | The Annual Cookie Tree: A Christmas Tradition — $15.00
SKU: 4095

A Drama Experience | The Messes We Make — $15.00
SKU: 5001

A Drama Experience | Who Let the Goat Out? — $15.00
SKU: 2049

Poetry - Collection 1 — $5.00
SKU: 6063

Six Syllables Drama — $10.00
SKU: 8035

CHILDREN'S BOOKS STUDY GUIDES

Buffalo Nickel Ranch | Study Guide — $0.00
SKU: 2082

Buggy Rides | Study Guide — $0.00
SKU: 2086

Daily Decisions - Who Let the Goat Out? — $5.00
SKU: 7012

Leaving Tracks | Study Guide — $0.00
SKU: 2084

The Cookie Tree | Study Guide — $0.00
SKU: 2085

Who Let The Goat Out | Study Guide — $0.00
SKU: 2083

CLASSROOM DECORATIONS

	Affirmation Station	Buffalo Nickel Ranch Theme SKU: 3021	$5.00
	Bathroom Pass	Buffalo Nickel Ranch Theme SKU: 3026	$1.00
	Birthdays Set	Buffalo Nickel Ranch Theme SKU: 3074	$7.00
	Blank Labels	Buffalo Nickel Ranch Theme SKU: 3076	$10.00
	Bulletin Board Border Set	Buffalo Nickel Ranch Theme SKU: 2045	$7.00
	Calendar Set	Buffalo Nickel Ranch Theme SKU: 3032	$7.00
	Color/Shape Posters	Buffalo Nickel Ranch Theme SKU: 3040	$7.00
	Cubby Labels	Buffalo Nickel Ranch Theme SKU: 3075	$15.00
	Drawer/Table Labels	Buffalo Nickel Ranch Theme SKU: 3072	$5.00

I can | Buffalo Nickel Ranch Theme SKU: 3041		$5.00
Jobs Chart | Buffalo Nickel Ranch Theme SKU: 6096		$5.00
Lowercase Alphabet | Buffalo Nickel Ranch Theme SKU: 3042		$15.00
Morning Meeting | Buffalo Nickel Ranch Theme SKU: 6095		$5.00
Nickel Number Charts 1-20 | Buffalo Nickel Ranch Theme SKU: 3043		$10.00
Sound Levels | Buffalo Nickel Ranch Theme SKU: 3055		$7.00
Sound Wall Bulletin Board Pieces | An effective way to begin this important Science of Reading process in a systematic way. SKU: 2081		$20.00
Uppercase + Lowercase Alphabet | Buffalo Nickel Ranch Theme SKU: 3056		$15.00
Wall Art | Buffalo Nickel Ranch Theme SKU: 3073		$10.00
Word Trio Page | Buffalo Nickel Ranch Theme SKU: 3057		$15.00

COLORATION ANNOTATION - CAPITALIZATION AND PUNCTUATION

	3rd Grade Coloration Annotation : Science - Capitalization & Punctuation SKU: 8057	$10.00
	4th Grade Coloration Annotation : Science - Capitalization & Punctuation SKU: 8053	$10.00
	5th Grade Coloration Annotation : Social Studies - Capitalization & Punctuation SKU: 8040	$10.00
	3rd Grade Coloration Annotation : Social Studies - Capitalization & Punctuation SKU: 8056	$10.00
	4th Grade Coloration Annotation : Social Studies - Capitalization & Punctuation SKU: 8048	$10.00
	5th Grade Coloration Annotation : Science - Capitalization & Punctuation SKU: 8043	$10.00

COLORATION ANNOTATION - GRAMMAR

	4th Grade Coloration Annotation : Social Studies - Grammar SKU: 8049	$10.00
	5th Grade Coloration Annotation : Social Studies - Grammar SKU: 8039	$10.00
	3rd Grade Coloration Annotation : Science - Grammar SKU: 8058	$10.00
	3rd Grade Coloration Annotation : Social Studies - Grammar SKU: 8055	$10.00
	4th Grade Coloration Annotation : Science - Grammar SKU: 8052	$10.00
	5th Grade Coloration Annotation : Science - Grammar SKU: 8041	$10.00

COLORATION ANNOTATION - PHONICS

4th Grade Coloration Annotation : Social Studies - Phonics $12.00
SKU: 8050

5th Grade Coloration Annotation : Social Studies - Phonics $12.00
SKU: 8038

3rd Grade Coloration Annotation : Science - Phonics $12.00
SKU: 8059

3rd Grade Coloration Annotation : Social Studies - Phonics $12.00
SKU: 8054

4th Grade Coloration Annotation : Science - Phonics $12.00
SKU: 8051

5th Grade Coloration Annotation : Science - Phonics $12.00
SKU: 8042

DIRECT DECODABLES

	Direct Decodable – The Dogs & The Bugs - Group 19 - Level A SKU: 8034	$2.00
	Direct Decodable – The Prettiest Animals - Group 20 - Level A SKU: 8033	$2.00
	Direct Decodable – Stella and Friends - Group 22 - Level A SKU: 8032	$2.00
	Direct Decodable – The Animals & Their Toys - Group 23 - Level A SKU: 8031	$2.00
	Direct Decodable – Girl and Horse - Group 21 - Level A SKU: 7094	$2.00
	Direct Decodable – The Cat Distrusts the Mouse - Group 18 - Level A SKU: 7093	$2.00
	Direct Decodable – Prepare the Dinner - Group 18 - Level A SKU: 7092	$2.00
	Direct Decodable – The Undone Bike - Group 18 - Level A SKU: 7091	$2.00
	Direct Decodable – Make the Return - Group 18 - Level A SKU: 7090	$2.00

Direct Decodable – The Boy - Group 17 - Level A **SKU:** 7089		$2.00
Direct Decodable – The Coin - Group 17 - Level A **SKU:** 7088		$2.00
Direct Decodable – Do You See the Cow? - Group 17 - Level A **SKU:** 7087		$2.00
Direct Decodable – We Will Look for You - Group 17 - Level A **SKU:** 7086		$2.00
Direct Decodable – We Will Look for You - Group 16 - Level A **SKU:** 7085		$2.00
Direct Decodable – The Good Book in the Pool - Group 16 - Level A **SKU:** 7084		$2.00
Direct Decodable – There's a Table in the Stable - Group 15 - Level A **SKU:** 7083		$2.00
Direct Decodable – The Monkey Has a Mother - Group 15 - Level A **SKU:** 7082		$2.00
Direct Decodable – The Swan Wants to Swim - Group 15 - Level A **SKU:** 7081		$2.00
Direct Decodable – It Has Been a Big Day - Group 15 - Level A **SKU:** 7080		$2.00
Direct Decodable – The Pig Went Home - Group 15 - Level A **SKU:** 7079		$2.00

Direct Decodable – My Friend is on the Field - Group 15 - Level A **SKU:** 7078		$2.00
Direct Decodable – He Said, She Said- Group 15 - Level A **SKU:** 7077		$2.00
Direct Decodable – The Bread - Group 15 - Level A **SKU:** 7076		$2.00
Direct Decodable – The Plaid Dress - Group 15 - Level A **SKU:** 7075		$2.00
Direct Decodable – The Boot and the Loot - Group 14 - Level A **SKU:** 7074		$2.00
Direct Decodable – True Blue - Group 14 - Level A **SKU:** 7073		$2.00
Direct Decodable – What Will We Do? - Group 14 - Level A **SKU:** 7072		$2.00
Direct Decodable – The Boat Floats - Group 14 - Level A **SKU:** 7071		$2.00
Direct Decodable – The Goat's Goal - Group 14 - Level A **SKU:** 7070		$2.00
Direct Decodable – The Snow Will Grow and Grow - Group 14 - Level A **SKU:** 7069		$2.00
Direct Decodable – Joe and the Goat - Group 14 - Level A **SKU:** 7068		$2.00

Direct Decodable – Joe and His Toe - Group 14 - Level A SKU: 7067		$2.00
Direct Decodable – I Like Pie - Group 14 - Level A SKU: 7066		$2.00
Direct Decodable – The Fly in the Sky - Group 14 - Level A SKU: 7065		$2.00
Direct Decodable – Reading is a Treat - Group 14 - Level A SKU: 7064		$2.00
Direct Decodable – The Key to Honey - Group 14 - Level A SKU: 7063		$2.00
Direct Decodable – He is Silly, Happy, and Funny - Group 14 - Level A SKU: 7062		$2.00
Direct Decodable – The Seed is Green - Group 14 - Level A SKU: 7061		$2.00
Direct Decodable – The Prey is Grey - Group 14 - Level A SKU: 7060		$2.00
Direct Decodable – They Play at the Bay - Group 14 - Level A SKU: 7059		$2.00
Direct Decodable – Going to the Farm - Group 13 - Level A SKU: 7058		$2.00
Direct Decodable – The Girl Will Help - Group 13 - Level A SKU: 7057		$2.00

Direct Decodable – The Sky is Dry - Group 12 - Level A SKU: 7056		$2.00
Direct Decodable – I Spy a Fly - Group 12 - Level A SKU: 7055		$2.00
Direct Decodable – The Elk - Group 11 - Level A SKU: 7054		$2.00
Direct Decodable – The Old Man, the Asp, and the Ant- Group 11 - Level A SKU: 7053		$2.00
Direct Decodable – The Bulldog and the Longhorn- Group 10 - Level A SKU: 7052		$2.00
Direct Decodable – Gems and Giants - Group 9 - Level A SKU: 7051		$2.00
Direct Decodable – Her Age - Group 9 - Level A SKU: 7050		$2.00
Direct Decodable – The Game at the Gym - Group 9 - Level A SKU: 7049		$2.00
Direct Decodable – The Cat at the Circus - Group 9 - Level A SKU: 7048		$2.00
Direct Decodable – Ace Can Run - Group 9 - Level A SKU: 7047		$2.00
Direct Decodable – Ice is on the Fence - Group 9 - Level A SKU: 7046		$2.00

Direct Decodable – The Fur - Group 8 - Level A SKU: 7045		$2.00
Direct Decodable – The Corn and the Thorn - Group 8 - Level A SKU: 7044		$2.00
Direct Decodable – The Girl Has a Skirt - Group 8 - Level A SKU: 7043		$2.00
Direct Decodable – I Hear With My Ear - Group 8 - Level A SKU: 7042		$2.00
Direct Decodable – The Herd and the Spider - Group 8 - Level A SKU: 7041		$2.00
Direct Decodable – Bill has a Car - Group 8 - Level A SKU: 7040		$2.00
Direct Decodable – There's a Barn on the Farm - Group 8 - Level A SKU: 7039		$2.00
Direct Decodable – The Bath - Group 7 - Level A SKU: 7038		$2.00
Direct Decodable – Champ and Chet - Group 7 - Level A SKU: 7037		$2.00
Direct Decodable – The Duck - Group 7 - Level A SKU: 7036		$2.00
Direct Decodable – Ink in the Sink - Group 7 - Level A SKU: 7035		$2.00

Direct Decodable – The King - Group 7 - Level A SKU: 7034		$2.00
Direct Decodable – Jeff and Jill - Group 6 - Level A SKU: 7033		$2.00
Direct Decodable – He Fell in a Well - Group 6 - Level A SKU: 7032		$2.00
Direct Decodable – Slim is Trim - Group 6 - Level A SKU: 7031		$2.00
Direct Decodable – The Grain Grew - Group 6 - Level A SKU: 7030		$2.00
Direct Decodable – Flags - Group 6 - Level A SKU: 7029		$2.00
Direct Decodable – The Tube is in the Cube - Group 5 - Level A SKU: 7028		$2.00
Direct Decodable – Big Box - Group 5 - Level A SKU: 7027		$2.00
Direct Decodable – Cats and Pups - Group 5 - Level A SKU: 7026		$2.00
Direct Decodable – Gus Has a Bus - Group 5 - Level A SKU: 7025		$2.00
Direct Decodable – Vets Like Pets - Group 4 - Level A SKU: 7024		$2.00

Direct Decodable – Pine Logs - Group 4 - Level A SKU: 7023		$2.00
Direct Decodable – Make a Cake - Group 4 - Level A SKU: 7022		$2.00
Direct Decodable – Spot the Dog - Group 4 - Level A SKU: 7021		$2.00
Direct Decodable – Hope on a Rope - Group 4 - Level A SKU: 7020		$2.00
Direct Decodable – Hogs Dig Holes - Group 4 - Level A SKU: 7019		$2.00
Direct Decodable – Hot Tots - Group 4 - Level A SKU: 7018		$2.00
Direct Decodable – He Rides a Wide Tide - Group 3 - Level A SKU: 7017		$2.00
Direct Decodable – The Pig Digs - Group 3 - Level A SKU: 7016		$2.00
Direct Decodable – Tim and Fin – Group 3 – Level A SKU: 7015		$2.00
Direct Decodable - Tim, Sam, and Tad - Group 3 - Level A SKU: 7014		$2.00
Direct Decodable - Jim and Ned - Group 3 - Level A SKU: 7013		$2.00

EDITING & REVISING

	Sentence Weather **SKU:** 2095	$15.00
	Sentence Weather - Interactive Weekly Forecast **SKU:** 6066	$10.00
	Supporting Rings for Editing & Revising **SKU:** 9037	$5.00
	TEKS Tribune - 3rd Grade Edition **SKU:** 6078	$3.00
	TEKS Tribune - 3rd Grade Edition - SPANISH **SKU:** 8044	$3.00
	TEKS Tribune - 4th Grade Edition **SKU:** 6079	$3.00
	TEKS Tribune - 4th Grade Edition - SPANISH **SKU:** 8045	$3.00
	TEKS Tribune - 5th Grade Edition **SKU:** 6080	$3.00
	TEKS Tribune - 5th Grade Edition - SPANISH **SKU:** 8046	$3.00

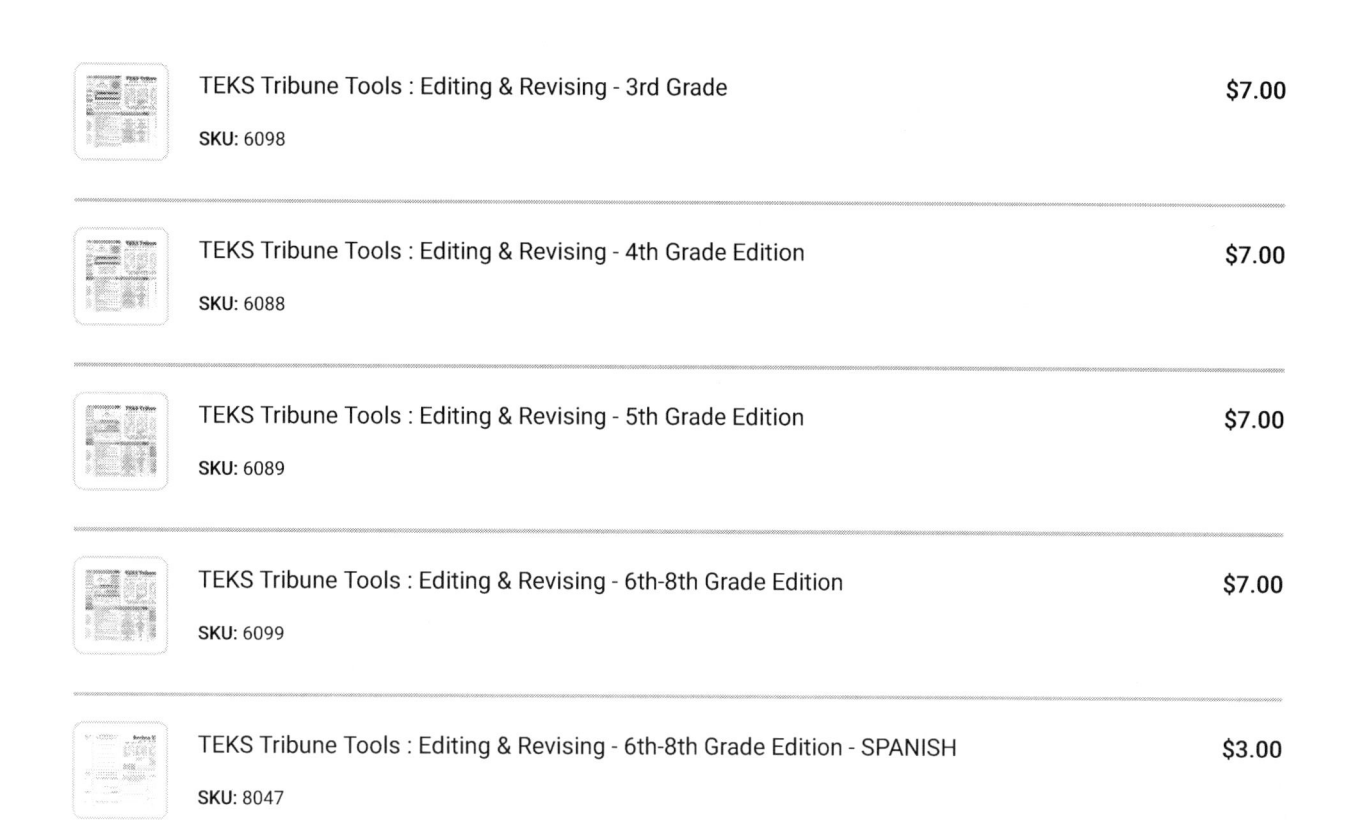

TEKS Tribune Tools : Editing & Revising - 3rd Grade **SKU:** 6098		$7.00
TEKS Tribune Tools : Editing & Revising - 4th Grade Edition **SKU:** 6088		$7.00
TEKS Tribune Tools : Editing & Revising - 5th Grade Edition **SKU:** 6089		$7.00
TEKS Tribune Tools : Editing & Revising - 6th-8th Grade Edition **SKU:** 6099		$7.00
TEKS Tribune Tools : Editing & Revising - 6th-8th Grade Edition - SPANISH **SKU:** 8047		$3.00

FUNDING DOCUMENTS

	Phonics Scope and Sequence Blueprint	This document contains a FREE blueprint of the Teach BIG Phonics Scope and Sequence. SKU: 2043	$0.00
	BIG Resources Online Practice Assessments - Instruction Guide & User Manual SKU: 7010	$0.00
	Digital Daily Classroom Lessons SKU: 3058	$0.00
	Make N Take Phonics Flyer SKU: 5082	$0.00
	Children's Book Magazine SKU: 5081	$0.00
	Author Order Form SKU: 3060	$0.00
	Children's Books Brochure SKU: 3059	$0.00
	Teach BIG Highly Acclaimed Staff SKU: 7011	$0.00
	**Mini Magazine	App** SKU: 4083	$0.00
	How To Schedule a Seminar SKU: 3061	$0.00

GRAMMAR

	1st Person vs 3rd Person Activity | This resource is great for grades 4-6. SKU: 2034	$2.00
	Adjective Postcards | This resource is great for grades 4-6. SKU: 2007	$5.00
	Adjective Word Search | This resource is great for grades 2-3. SKU: 2003	$2.00
	Advertising with Purpose - Ethos, Logos, Pathos | This resource is great for grades 7-8. SKU: 2031	$5.00
	Alliteration Ambrosia Activity | This resource is great for grades 4-6. SKU: 2015	$5.00
	Antonym Acting! | This resource is great for grades 2-3. SKU: 2014	$5.00
	Author's Purpose Game Board | This resource is great for grades 4-6. SKU: 1099	$5.00
	Capitalization Trashketball Activity | This resource is great for grades 2-3. SKU: 1098	$5.00
	Capitalizing Proper Nouns | This resource is great for grades 4-6. SKU: 2006	$1.00

Contraction Puzzles Activity | This resource is great for grades 2-3. SKU: 2002		$2.00
Correlative Conjunctions | This resource is great for grades 4-6. SKU: 2018		$5.00
Counter Arguments | This resource is great for grades 7-8. SKU: 2033		$2.00
Fairy-Tale Characteristics | This resource is great for grades 2-3. SKU: 2030		$5.00
Homophone Crossword | This resource is great for grades 4-6. SKU: 1097		$2.00
Literary Devices Bingo | This resource is great for grades 7-8. SKU: 1095		$7.00
Marking the Punctuation | This resource is great for grades 4-6. SKU: 2035		$2.00
Memorize It! | This resource is great for grades 7-8. SKU: 2022		$2.00
Missing Punctuation Activity | This resource is great for grades 4-6. SKU: 1096		$2.00
Parts of Speech Activity | This resource is great for grades 2-3. SKU: 2012		$7.00
Phonemes Haircuts Activity | This resource is great for grades 2-3. SKU: 2004		$2.00

Plural Pies	This resource is great for grades 4-6. **SKU:** 2024	$1.00
Prepositions "4 in a Row" Activity	This resource is great for grades 7-8. **SKU:** 2010	$2.00
Punting Punctuation Activity	This resource is great for grades 7-8. **SKU:** 2011	$7.00
Rhyme Schemes	This resource is great for grades 2-3. **SKU:** 2027	$1.00
Rolling Personifications Activity	This resource is great for grades 7-8. **SKU:** 2000	$1.00
Rounding Up The Nouns	This resource is great for grades 4-6. **SKU:** 2016	$2.00
Sentence Weather - Interactive Weekly Forecast **SKU:** 6066	$10.00
Singular & Plural Nouns Cookies Activity	This resource is great for grades 2-3. **SKU:** 2005	$5.00
Storytelling Adverbs	This resource is great for grades 7-8. **SKU:** 2032	$2.00
Thesis Tic Tac Toe	This resource is great for grades 4-6. **SKU:** 2026	$5.00
Verb Tents Activity	This resource is great for grades 7-8. **SKU:** 2009	$5.00

"Looking into the Future" Foreshadowing Activity | This resource is great for grades 7-8.　　　　$2.00

SKU: 2017

"Stop Running" Run-on Sentences Activity | This resource is great for grades 7-8.　　　　$5.00

SKU: 2019

HIGH FREQUENCY WORD BOOKLETS

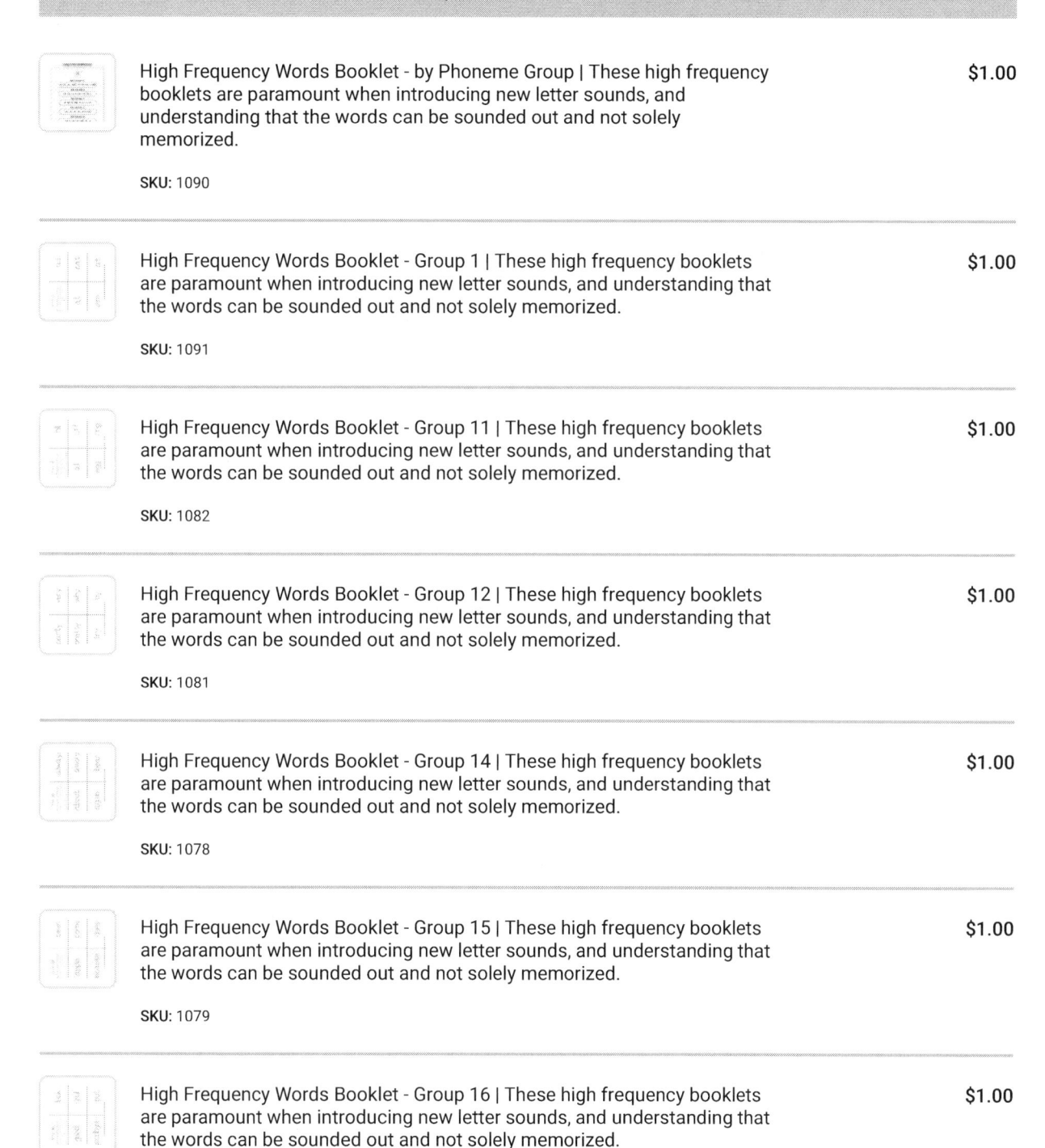

High Frequency Words Booklet - by Phoneme Group | These high frequency booklets are paramount when introducing new letter sounds, and understanding that the words can be sounded out and not solely memorized.　　　　$1.00

SKU: 1090

High Frequency Words Booklet - Group 1 | These high frequency booklets are paramount when introducing new letter sounds, and understanding that the words can be sounded out and not solely memorized.　　　　$1.00

SKU: 1091

High Frequency Words Booklet - Group 11 | These high frequency booklets are paramount when introducing new letter sounds, and understanding that the words can be sounded out and not solely memorized.　　　　$1.00

SKU: 1082

High Frequency Words Booklet - Group 12 | These high frequency booklets are paramount when introducing new letter sounds, and understanding that the words can be sounded out and not solely memorized.　　　　$1.00

SKU: 1081

High Frequency Words Booklet - Group 14 | These high frequency booklets are paramount when introducing new letter sounds, and understanding that the words can be sounded out and not solely memorized.　　　　$1.00

SKU: 1078

High Frequency Words Booklet - Group 15 | These high frequency booklets are paramount when introducing new letter sounds, and understanding that the words can be sounded out and not solely memorized.　　　　$1.00

SKU: 1079

High Frequency Words Booklet - Group 16 | These high frequency booklets are paramount when introducing new letter sounds, and understanding that the words can be sounded out and not solely memorized.　　　　$1.00

SKU: 1077

High Frequency Words Booklet - Group 17 | These high frequency booklets are paramount when introducing new letter sounds, and understanding that the words can be sounded out and not solely memorized. **SKU:** 1080		$1.00
High Frequency Words Booklet - Group 2 | These high frequency booklets are paramount when introducing new letter sounds, and understanding that the words can be sounded out and not solely memorized. **SKU:** 1089		$1.00
High Frequency Words Booklet - Group 3 | These high frequency booklets are paramount when introducing new letter sounds, and understanding that the words can be sounded out and not solely memorized. **SKU:** 1088		$1.00
High Frequency Words Booklet - Group 4 | These high frequency booklets are paramount when introducing new letter sounds, and understanding that the words can be sounded out and not solely memorized. **SKU:** 1087		$1.00
High Frequency Words Booklet - Group 5 | These high frequency booklets are paramount when introducing new letter sounds, and understanding that the words can be sounded out and not solely memorized. **SKU:** 1086		$1.00
High Frequency Words Booklet - Group 6 | These high frequency booklets are paramount when introducing new letter sounds, and understanding that the words can be sounded out and not solely memorized. **SKU:** 1085		$1.00
High Frequency Words Booklet - Group 7 | These high frequency booklets are paramount when introducing new letter sounds, and understanding that the words can be sounded out and not solely memorized. **SKU:** 1084		$1.00
High Frequency Words Booklet - Group 8 | These high frequency booklets are paramount when introducing new letter sounds, and understanding that the words can be sounded out and not solely memorized. **SKU:** 1083		$1.00
High Frequency Words Booklet - Outliers | These high frequency booklets are paramount when introducing new letter sounds, and understanding that the words can be sounded out and not solely memorized. **SKU:** 1092		$1.00

HOME TO SCHOOL LETTERS | SPANISH

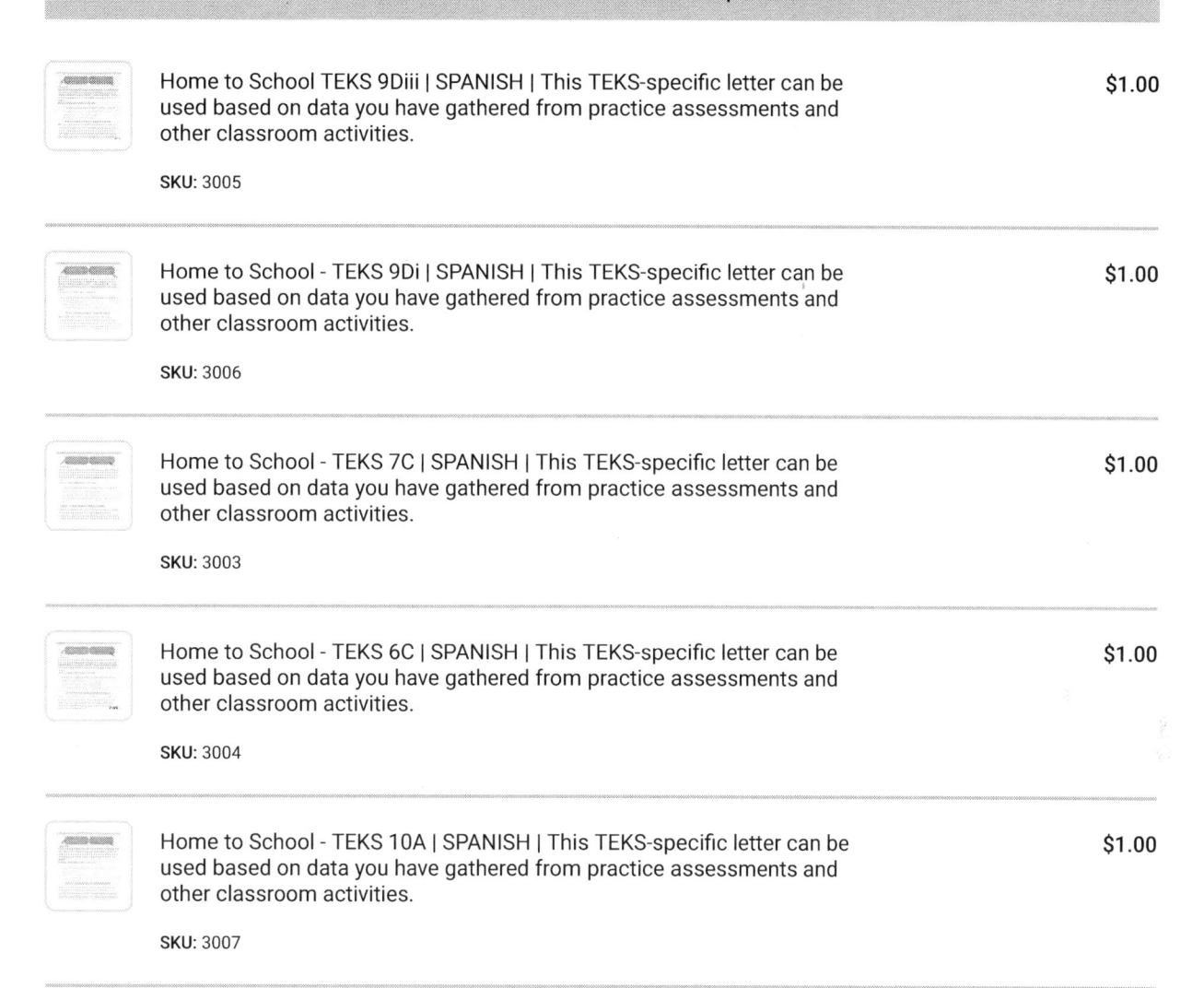

Home to School TEKS 9Diii | SPANISH | This TEKS-specific letter can be used based on data you have gathered from practice assessments and other classroom activities. $1.00

SKU: 3005

Home to School - TEKS 9Di | SPANISH | This TEKS-specific letter can be used based on data you have gathered from practice assessments and other classroom activities. $1.00

SKU: 3006

Home to School - TEKS 7C | SPANISH | This TEKS-specific letter can be used based on data you have gathered from practice assessments and other classroom activities. $1.00

SKU: 3003

Home to School - TEKS 6C | SPANISH | This TEKS-specific letter can be used based on data you have gathered from practice assessments and other classroom activities. $1.00

SKU: 3004

Home to School - TEKS 10A | SPANISH | This TEKS-specific letter can be used based on data you have gathered from practice assessments and other classroom activities. $1.00

SKU: 3007

KINDERGARTEN TEKS LESSON PLANS

	Kindergarten	Unit 2: Text Connections SKU: 5021	$20.00
	Kindergarten	Unit 8A: Informational Text SKU: 5076	$20.00
	Kindergarten	Unit 7A: Drama SKU: 5074	$20.00
	Kindergarten	Unit 3: Generating Questions SKU: 5022	$20.00
	Kindergarten	Unit 1: Literary Foundations SKU: 4050	$20.00
	Kindergarten	Unit 11: Bringing It All Together SKU: 5080	$20.00
	Kindergarten	Unit 10: Persuasive Text SKU: 5079	$20.00
	Kindergarten	Unit 9: Poetry SKU: 5078	$20.00
	Kindergarten	Unit 8B: Diving Further into Informational SKU: 5077	$20.00

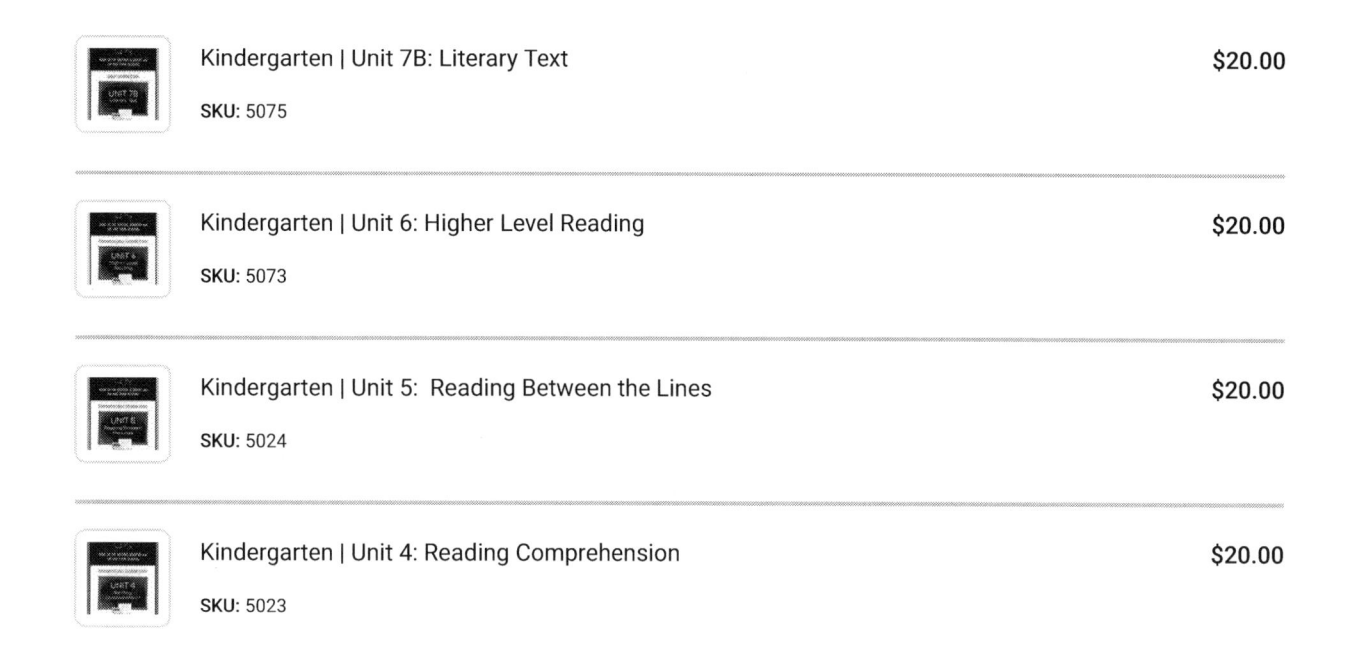

	Kindergarten	Unit 7B: Literary Text **SKU:** 5075	$20.00
	Kindergarten	Unit 6: Higher Level Reading **SKU:** 5073	$20.00
	Kindergarten	Unit 5: Reading Between the Lines **SKU:** 5024	$20.00
	Kindergarten	Unit 4: Reading Comprehension **SKU:** 5023	$20.00

LAPBOOK FOLDABLES

STAAR Lapbook Foldable - Chocolate Chip Cookies — $7.00
SKU: 3077

STAAR Lapbook Foldable - Chocolate Chip Cookies | SPANISH — $7.00
SKU: 3083

LETTER READERS

	Letter Readers - Group 1 (m,t,s,r,c,a)	Each Letter Reader book focuses only on the letters from that particular group within the scope and sequence. This promotes a systemic approach to teaching using the Science of Reading research. **SKU:** 1050	$2.00
	Letter Readers Bundle	Each Letter Reader book focuses only on the letters from that particular group within the scope and sequence. This promotes a systemic approach to teaching using the Science of Reading research. **SKU:** 2059	$7.00
	Letter Readers – Group 2 (B,H,D, Long a,e)	Each Letter Reader book focuses only on the letters from that particular group within the scope and sequence. This promotes a systemic approach to teaching using the Science of Reading research. **SKU:** 1052	$2.00
	Letter Readers – Group 3 (n,w,p,j,f)	Each Letter Reader book focuses only on the letters from that particular group within the scope and sequence. This promotes a systemic approach to teaching using the Science of Reading research. **SKU:** 1051	$2.00
	Letter Readers – Group 4 (g,k,l,v,o)	Each Letter Reader book focuses only on the letters from that particular group within the scope and sequence. This promotes a systemic approach to teaching using the Science of Reading research. **SKU:** 1053	$2.00
	Letter Readers – Group 5 (x,y,z,q,u)	Each Letter Reader book focuses only on the letters from that particular group within the scope and sequence. This promotes a systemic approach to teaching using the Science of Reading research. **SKU:** 1054	$2.00

ONLINE ASSESSMENT PLATFORM

Level A, B, C SKU: 2098	**Visit teachbig.com or teachbigapp.com for pricing information**	$0.00

PAIRED PASSAGES

Solar Eclipse Paired Passages : Set 3 – 3th-5th Grade SKU: 8063		$5.00
Argumentative Paired Passages : Set 1 - 3rd - 5th Grade SKU: 6056		$5.00
Solar Eclipse Paired Passages : Set 3 – 6th - 8th Grade SKU: 8064		$5.00
Solar Eclipse Paired Passages : Set 3 – 9th - 10th Grade SKU: 8065		$5.00
March Madness Paired Passages : Set 2 – 3rd - 5th Grade SKU: 8061		$5.00
Argumentative Paired Passages : Set 1 - 6th - 8th Grade SKU: 6057		$5.00
March Madness Paired Passages : Set 2 – 9th - 10th Grade SKU: 8060		$5.00

March Madness Paired Passages : Set 2 – 6th - 8th Grade $5.00

SKU: 8062

Argumentative Paired Passages : Set 1 – 9th - 10th Grade $5.00

SKU: 6058

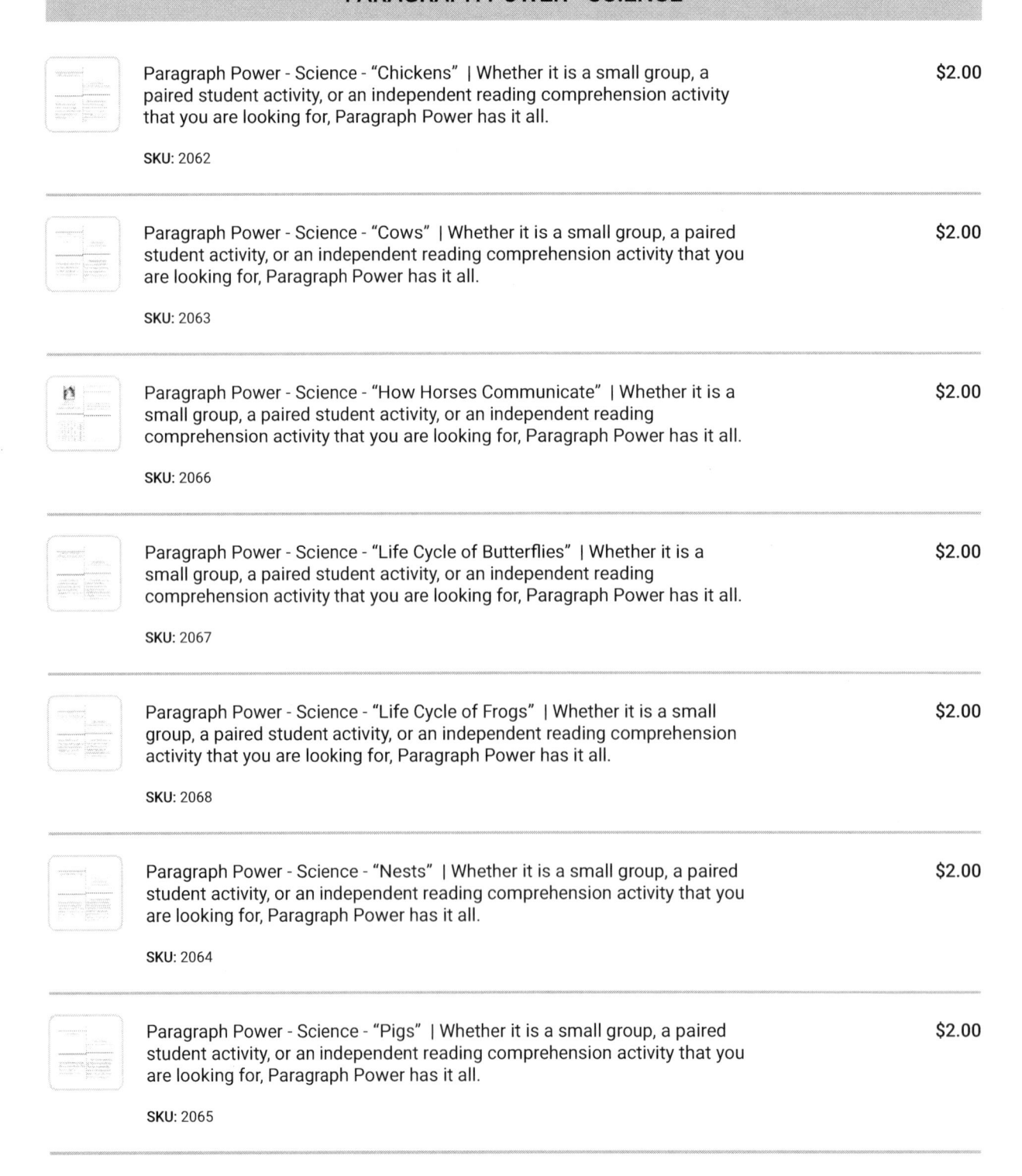

PARAGRAPH POWER - SCIENCE

Paragraph Power - Science - "Chickens" | Whether it is a small group, a paired student activity, or an independent reading comprehension activity that you are looking for, Paragraph Power has it all. — $2.00

SKU: 2062

Paragraph Power - Science - "Cows" | Whether it is a small group, a paired student activity, or an independent reading comprehension activity that you are looking for, Paragraph Power has it all. — $2.00

SKU: 2063

Paragraph Power - Science - "How Horses Communicate" | Whether it is a small group, a paired student activity, or an independent reading comprehension activity that you are looking for, Paragraph Power has it all. — $2.00

SKU: 2066

Paragraph Power - Science - "Life Cycle of Butterflies" | Whether it is a small group, a paired student activity, or an independent reading comprehension activity that you are looking for, Paragraph Power has it all. — $2.00

SKU: 2067

Paragraph Power - Science - "Life Cycle of Frogs" | Whether it is a small group, a paired student activity, or an independent reading comprehension activity that you are looking for, Paragraph Power has it all. — $2.00

SKU: 2068

Paragraph Power - Science - "Nests" | Whether it is a small group, a paired student activity, or an independent reading comprehension activity that you are looking for, Paragraph Power has it all. — $2.00

SKU: 2064

Paragraph Power - Science - "Pigs" | Whether it is a small group, a paired student activity, or an independent reading comprehension activity that you are looking for, Paragraph Power has it all. — $2.00

SKU: 2065

Paragraph Power - Science - "Trees"	Whether it is a small group, a paired student activity, or an independent reading comprehension activity that you are looking for, Paragraph Power has it all. SKU: 2069	$2.00
Paragraph Power – Science "Astronomy"	Whether it is a small group, a paired student activity, or an independent reading comprehension activity that you are looking for, Paragraph Power has it all. SKU: 4043	$2.00
Paragraph Power – Science "Habitats"	Whether it is a small group, a paired student activity, or an independent reading comprehension activity that you are looking for, Paragraph Power has it all. SKU: 4042	$2.00
Paragraph Power – Science "Instruments"	Whether it is a small group, a paired student activity, or an independent reading comprehension activity that you are looking for, Paragraph Power has it all. SKU: 4046	$2.00
Paragraph Power – Science "Moon Phases"	Whether it is a small group, a paired student activity, or an independent reading comprehension activity that you are looking for, Paragraph Power has it all. SKU: 4044	$2.00
Paragraph Power – Science "The Lifecycle of Frogs"	Whether it is a small group, a paired student activity, or an independent reading comprehension activity that you are looking for, Paragraph Power has it all. SKU: 4048	$2.00
Paragraph Power – Science "Water Cycle"	Whether it is a small group, a paired student activity, or an independent reading comprehension activity that you are looking for, Paragraph Power has it all. SKU: 4045	$2.00
Paragraph Power – Science "Weather"	Whether it is a small group, a paired student activity, or an independent reading comprehension activity that you are looking for, Paragraph Power has it all. SKU: 4047	$2.00

PARAGRAPH POWER - SCIENCE - BUNDLES

Paragraph Power : Science – Bundle 3 | Whether it is a small group, a paired student activity, or an independent reading comprehension activity that you are looking for, Paragraph Power has it all. $8.00

SKU: 8067

Paragraph Power : Science – Bundle 2 | Whether it is a small group, a paired student activity, or an independent reading comprehension activity that you are looking for, Paragraph Power has it all. $8.00

SKU: 8066

Paragraph Power : Science – Bundle 1 | Whether it is a small group, a paired student activity, or an independent reading comprehension activity that you are looking for, Paragraph Power has it all. $8.00

SKU: 6062

PARAGRAPH POWER - SOCIAL STUDIES

Paragraph Power - Social Studies - "Blue Bonnets" | Whether it is a small group, a paired student activity, or an independent reading comprehension activity that you are looking for, Paragraph Power has it all. — $2.00

SKU: 2073

Paragraph Power - Social Studies - "Collecting Coins" | Whether it is a small group, a paired student activity, or an independent reading comprehension activity that you are looking for, Paragraph Power has it all. — $2.00

SKU: 2074

Paragraph Power - Social Studies - "Community Helpers" | Whether it is a small group, a paired student activity, or an independent reading comprehension activity that you are looking for, Paragraph Power has it all. — $2.00

SKU: 2070

Paragraph Power - Social Studies - "Family Traditions" | Whether it is a small group, a paired student activity, or an independent reading comprehension activity that you are looking for, Paragraph Power has it all. — $2.00

SKU: 2075

Paragraph Power - Social Studies - "Importance of Farming" | Whether it is a small group, a paired student activity, or an independent reading comprehension activity that you are looking for, Paragraph Power has it all. — $2.00

SKU: 2076

Paragraph Power - Social Studies - "Importance of Maps" | Whether it is a small group, a paired student activity, or an independent reading comprehension activity that you are looking for, Paragraph Power has it all. — $2.00

SKU: 2077

Paragraph Power - Social Studies - "Instruments" | Whether it is a small group, a paired student activity, or an independent reading comprehension activity that you are looking for, Paragraph Power has it all. — $2.00

SKU: 2078

Paragraph Power - Social Studies - "Invention of Lamps"	Whether it is a small group, a paired student activity, or an independent reading comprehension activity that you are looking for, Paragraph Power has it all. **SKU:** 2079	$2.00
Paragraph Power - Social Studies - "July 4th"	Whether it is a small group, a paired student activity, or an independent reading comprehension activity that you are looking for, Paragraph Power has it all. **SKU:** 2080	$2.00
Paragraph Power - Social Studies - "Texas Flag"	Whether it is a small group, a paired student activity, or an independent reading comprehension activity that you are looking for, Paragraph Power has it all. **SKU:** 2071	$2.00
Paragraph Power - Social Studies - "Transportation"	Whether it is a small group, a paired student activity, or an independent reading comprehension activity that you are looking for, Paragraph Power has it all. **SKU:** 2072	$2.00

PARAGRAPH POWER - SOCIAL STUDIES - BUNDLES

Paragraph Power : Social Studies – Bundle 2	Whether it is a small group, a paired student activity, or an independent reading comprehension activity that you are looking for, Paragraph Power has it all. **SKU:** 8069	$8.00
Paragraph Power : Social Studies – Bundle 1	Whether it is a small group, a paired student activity, or an independent reading comprehension activity that you are looking for, Paragraph Power has it all. **SKU:** 8068	$8.00

PARENT COMMUNICATION

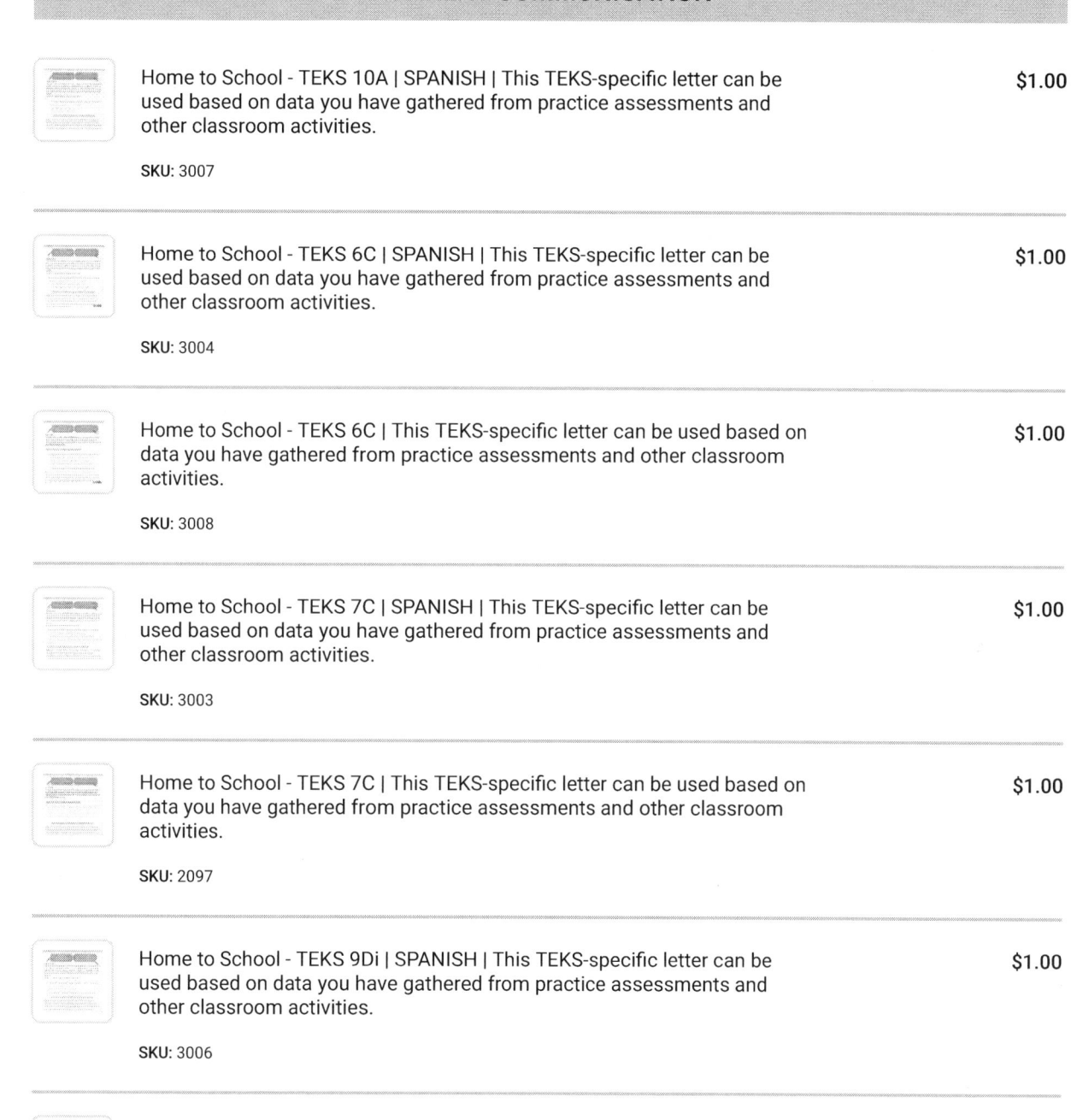

Home to School - TEKS 10A	SPANISH	This TEKS-specific letter can be used based on data you have gathered from practice assessments and other classroom activities. **SKU:** 3007	$1.00
Home to School - TEKS 6C	SPANISH	This TEKS-specific letter can be used based on data you have gathered from practice assessments and other classroom activities. **SKU:** 3004	$1.00
Home to School - TEKS 6C	This TEKS-specific letter can be used based on data you have gathered from practice assessments and other classroom activities. **SKU:** 3008	$1.00
Home to School - TEKS 7C	SPANISH	This TEKS-specific letter can be used based on data you have gathered from practice assessments and other classroom activities. **SKU:** 3003	$1.00
Home to School - TEKS 7C	This TEKS-specific letter can be used based on data you have gathered from practice assessments and other classroom activities. **SKU:** 2097	$1.00
Home to School - TEKS 9Di	SPANISH	This TEKS-specific letter can be used based on data you have gathered from practice assessments and other classroom activities. **SKU:** 3006	$1.00
Home to School - TEKS 9Di	This TEKS-specific letter can be used based on data you have gathered from practice assessments and other classroom activities. **SKU:** 3010	$1.00

Home to School - TEKS 9Diii | This TEKS-specific letter can be used based on data you have gathered from practice assessments and other classroom activities.

SKU: 3009

$1.00

Home to School TEKS 10A | This TEKS-specific letter can be used based on data you have gathered from practice assessments and other classroom activities.

SKU: 3011

$1.00

Home to School TEKS 9Diii | SPANISH | This TEKS-specific letter can be used based on data you have gathered from practice assessments and other classroom activities.

SKU: 3005

$1.00

PARENT LETTERS

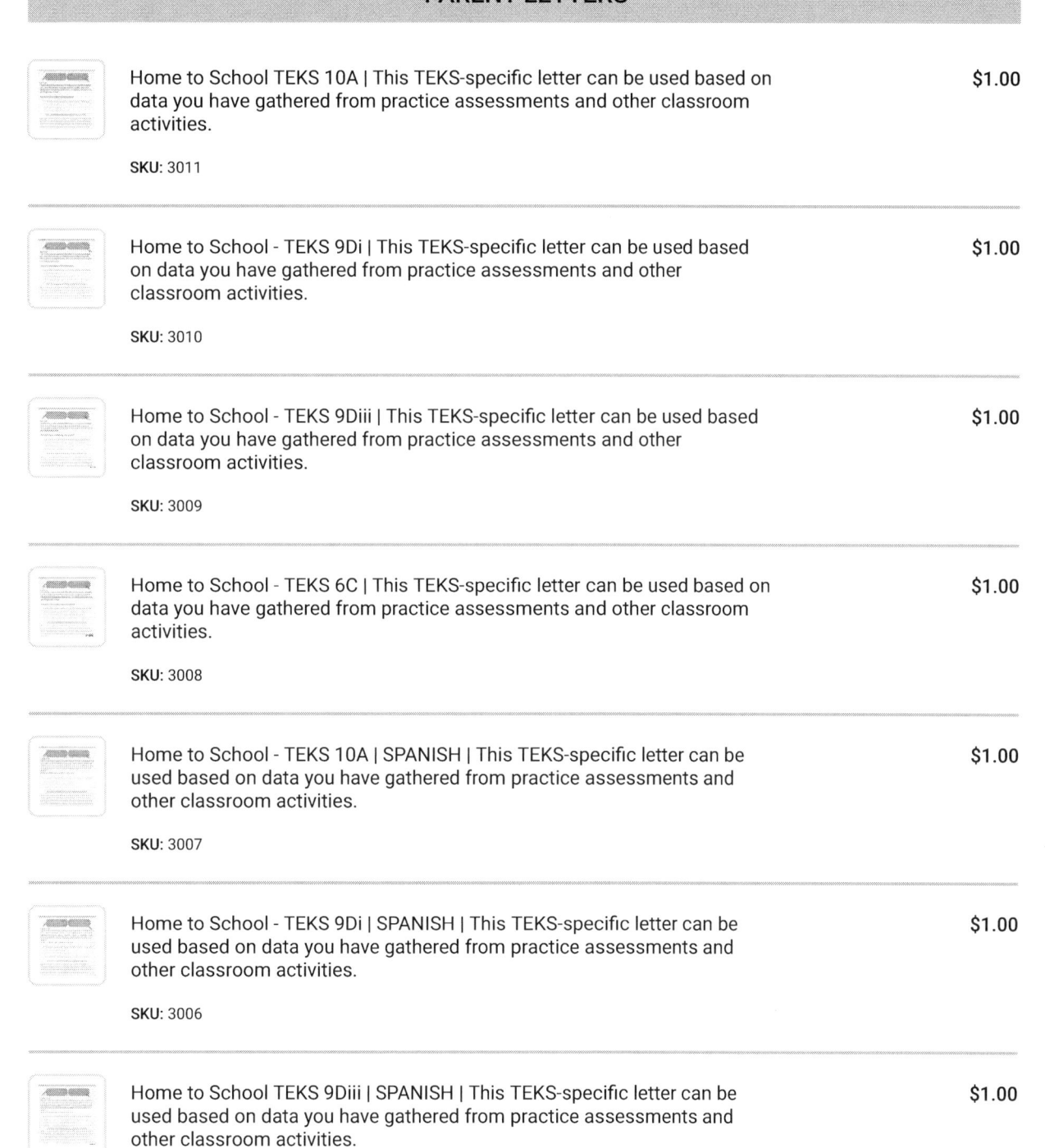

	Home to School TEKS 10A	This TEKS-specific letter can be used based on data you have gathered from practice assessments and other classroom activities. **SKU:** 3011	$1.00
	Home to School - TEKS 9Di	This TEKS-specific letter can be used based on data you have gathered from practice assessments and other classroom activities. **SKU:** 3010	$1.00
	Home to School - TEKS 9Diii	This TEKS-specific letter can be used based on data you have gathered from practice assessments and other classroom activities. **SKU:** 3009	$1.00
	Home to School - TEKS 6C	This TEKS-specific letter can be used based on data you have gathered from practice assessments and other classroom activities. **SKU:** 3008	$1.00
	Home to School - TEKS 10A	SPANISH	This TEKS-specific letter can be used based on data you have gathered from practice assessments and other classroom activities. **SKU:** 3007	$1.00
	Home to School - TEKS 9Di	SPANISH	This TEKS-specific letter can be used based on data you have gathered from practice assessments and other classroom activities. **SKU:** 3006	$1.00
	Home to School TEKS 9Diii	SPANISH	This TEKS-specific letter can be used based on data you have gathered from practice assessments and other classroom activities. **SKU:** 3005	$1.00

	Home to School - TEKS 6C | SPANISH | This TEKS-specific letter can be used based on data you have gathered from practice assessments and other classroom activities. **SKU:** 3004	$1.00
	Home to School - TEKS 7C | SPANISH | This TEKS-specific letter can be used based on data you have gathered from practice assessments and other classroom activities. **SKU:** 3003	$1.00
	Home to School - TEKS 7C | This TEKS-specific letter can be used based on data you have gathered from practice assessments and other classroom activities. **SKU:** 2097	$1.00

PARENTS

	Sound Blocks for Home **SKU:** 9036	$12.00

PHONICS

15 Common Phonics Rules Poster Set — $0.00
SKU: 2087

Adjective Word Trios | The additive word trios item is a set of 36 sets of three words that cover all of the adjective types. — $15.00
SKU: 2047

All The Ways to Spell Long Vowel Sounds | This useful document contains all of the different spellings/letter arrangements (graphemes) that make up the vowel sounds (vowel phonemes). — $5.00
SKU: 2046

Alphabet & Phoneme Booklets | The alphabet and phenome booklets serve many Science & Reading phonics purposes. These can be used by a whole group, small group, in stations, individually, or for at-home purposes. — $20.00
SKU: 1094

Alphabet Mouth Shapes | Flashcards — $5.00
SKU: 4067

Alphabet Mouth Shapes | Full Sheet — $5.00
SKU: 4065

Alphabet Mouth Shapes | Half Sheets — $5.00
SKU: 4066

Attention to Comprehension — $12.00
SKU: 9035

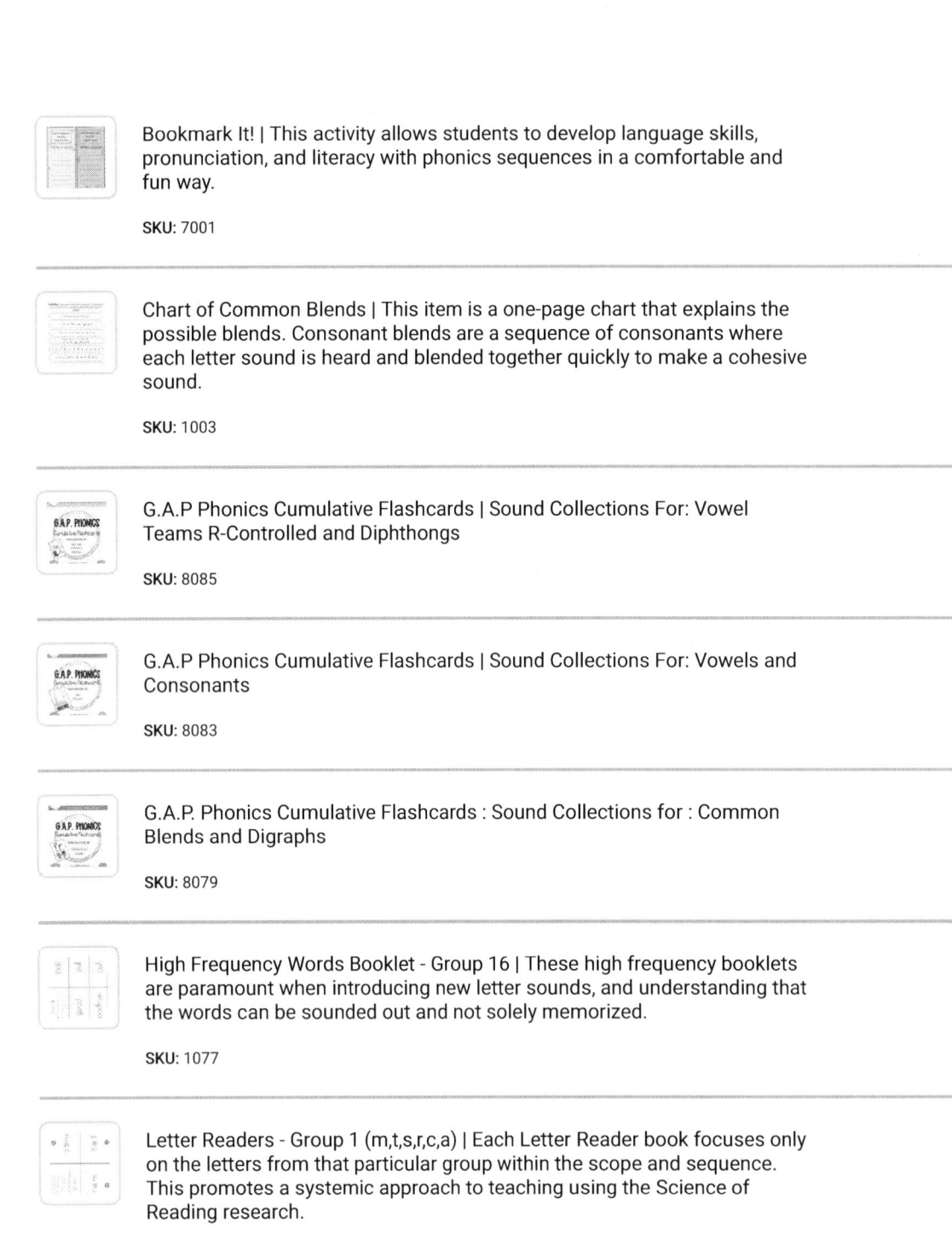

	Bookmark It!	This activity allows students to develop language skills, pronunciation, and literacy with phonics sequences in a comfortable and fun way. **SKU:** 7001	$5.00
	Chart of Common Blends	This item is a one-page chart that explains the possible blends. Consonant blends are a sequence of consonants where each letter sound is heard and blended together quickly to make a cohesive sound. **SKU:** 1003	$1.00
	G.A.P Phonics Cumulative Flashcards	Sound Collections For: Vowel Teams R-Controlled and Diphthongs **SKU:** 8085	$12.00
	G.A.P Phonics Cumulative Flashcards	Sound Collections For: Vowels and Consonants **SKU:** 8083	$12.00
	G.A.P. Phonics Cumulative Flashcards : Sound Collections for : Common Blends and Digraphs **SKU:** 8079	$12.00
	High Frequency Words Booklet - Group 16	These high frequency booklets are paramount when introducing new letter sounds, and understanding that the words can be sounded out and not solely memorized. **SKU:** 1077	$1.00
	Letter Readers - Group 1 (m,t,s,r,c,a)	Each Letter Reader book focuses only on the letters from that particular group within the scope and sequence. This promotes a systemic approach to teaching using the Science of Reading research. **SKU:** 1050	$2.00
	Letter Readers – Group 2 (B,H,D, Long a,e)	Each Letter Reader book focuses only on the letters from that particular group within the scope and sequence. This promotes a systemic approach to teaching using the Science of Reading research. **SKU:** 1052	$2.00
	Letter Readers – Group 3 (n,w,p,j,f)	Each Letter Reader book focuses only on the letters from that particular group within the scope and sequence. This promotes a systemic approach to teaching using the Science of Reading research. **SKU:** 1051	$2.00

	Letter Readers – Group 4 (g,k,l,v,o)	Each Letter Reader book focuses only on the letters from that particular group within the scope and sequence. This promotes a systemic approach to teaching using the Science of Reading research. SKU: 1053	$2.00
	Letter Readers – Group 5 (x,y,z,q,u)	Each Letter Reader book focuses only on the letters from that particular group within the scope and sequence. This promotes a systemic approach to teaching using the Science of Reading research. SKU: 1054	$2.00
	Letter Sound Tiles	The Letter Sound Tiles provide an auditory, visual, and kinesthetic approach to learning and utilizing letter sounds in order to create words. SKU: 2044	$15.00
	Paragraph Power - Science - "Chickens"	Whether it is a small group, a paired student activity, or an independent reading comprehension activity that you are looking for, Paragraph Power has it all. SKU: 2062	$2.00
	Paragraph Power - Science - "Cows"	Whether it is a small group, a paired student activity, or an independent reading comprehension activity that you are looking for, Paragraph Power has it all. SKU: 2063	$2.00
	Paragraph Power - Science - "Life Cycle of Butterflies"	Whether it is a small group, a paired student activity, or an independent reading comprehension activity that you are looking for, Paragraph Power has it all. SKU: 2067	$2.00
	Paragraph Power - Science - "Life Cycle of Frogs"	Whether it is a small group, a paired student activity, or an independent reading comprehension activity that you are looking for, Paragraph Power has it all. SKU: 2068	$2.00
	Paragraph Power - Science - "Nests"	Whether it is a small group, a paired student activity, or an independent reading comprehension activity that you are looking for, Paragraph Power has it all. SKU: 2064	$2.00

Paragraph Power - Science - "Pigs"	Whether it is a small group, a paired student activity, or an independent reading comprehension activity that you are looking for, Paragraph Power has it all. **SKU:** 2065	$2.00
Paragraph Power - Science - "Trees"	Whether it is a small group, a paired student activity, or an independent reading comprehension activity that you are looking for, Paragraph Power has it all. **SKU:** 2069	$2.00
Paragraph Power - Social Studies - "Blue Bonnets"	Whether it is a small group, a paired student activity, or an independent reading comprehension activity that you are looking for, Paragraph Power has it all. **SKU:** 2073	$2.00
Paragraph Power - Social Studies - "Collecting Coins"	Whether it is a small group, a paired student activity, or an independent reading comprehension activity that you are looking for, Paragraph Power has it all. **SKU:** 2074	$2.00
Paragraph Power - Social Studies - "Community Helpers"	Whether it is a small group, a paired student activity, or an independent reading comprehension activity that you are looking for, Paragraph Power has it all. **SKU:** 2070	$2.00
Paragraph Power - Social Studies - "Family Traditions"	Whether it is a small group, a paired student activity, or an independent reading comprehension activity that you are looking for, Paragraph Power has it all. **SKU:** 2075	$2.00
Paragraph Power - Social Studies - "Importance of Farming"	Whether it is a small group, a paired student activity, or an independent reading comprehension activity that you are looking for, Paragraph Power has it all. **SKU:** 2076	$2.00
Paragraph Power - Social Studies - "Importance of Maps"	Whether it is a small group, a paired student activity, or an independent reading comprehension activity that you are looking for, Paragraph Power has it all. **SKU:** 2077	$2.00
Paragraph Power - Social Studies - "Instruments"	Whether it is a small group, a paired student activity, or an independent reading comprehension activity that you are looking for, Paragraph Power has it all. **SKU:** 2078	$2.00

	Paragraph Power - Social Studies - "Invention of Lamps"	Whether it is a small group, a paired student activity, or an independent reading comprehension activity that you are looking for, Paragraph Power has it all. SKU: 2079	$2.00
	Paragraph Power - Social Studies - "July 4th"	Whether it is a small group, a paired student activity, or an independent reading comprehension activity that you are looking for, Paragraph Power has it all. SKU: 2080	$2.00
	Paragraph Power - Social Studies - "Texas Flag"	Whether it is a small group, a paired student activity, or an independent reading comprehension activity that you are looking for, Paragraph Power has it all. SKU: 2071	$2.00
	Paragraph Power - Social Studies - "Transportation"	Whether it is a small group, a paired student activity, or an independent reading comprehension activity that you are looking for, Paragraph Power has it all. SKU: 2072	$2.00
	Phonics Definitions Part 1	This document contains common phonics words and definitions. SKU: 2048	$0.00
	Phonics Phonemes & Graphemes Poster Set	This poster set contains all of the leading phonics systematic rules. SKU: 8000	$30.00
	Phonics Scope and Sequence Blueprint	This document contains a FREE blueprint of the Teach BIG Phonics Scope and Sequence. SKU: 2043	$0.00
	Phonogram Flashcards SKU: 4049	$15.00
	Selection Collection - Science - "Pigs"	Included in the Selection Collection, you will find a nonfiction, fiction, poetry, and drama passage. SKU: 2057	$5.00
	Selection Collection - Science - "Spiders"	Included in the Selection Collection, you will find a nonfiction, fiction, poetry, and drama passage. SKU: 2056	$5.00

	Selection Collection - Social Studies - "Blue Bonnet"	Included in the Selection Collection, you will find a nonfiction, fiction, poetry, and drama passage. **SKU:** 2053	$5.00
	Selection Collection - Social Studies - "Collecting Coins"	Included in the Selection Collection, you will find a nonfiction, fiction, poetry, and drama passage. **SKU:** 2051	$5.00
	Selection Collection - Social Studies - "Invention of Toilet Paper"	Included in the Selection Collection, you will find a nonfiction, fiction, poetry, and drama passage. **SKU:** 2050	$5.00
	Selection Collection - Social Studies - "Johnny Appleseed"	Included in the Selection Collection, you will find a nonfiction, fiction, poetry, and drama passage. **SKU:** 2055	$5.00
	Selection Collection - Social Studies - "Texas Flag"	Included in the Selection Collection, you will find a nonfiction, fiction, poetry, and drama passage. **SKU:** 2052	$5.00
	Selection Collection - Social Studies - "Transportation"	Included in the Selection Collection, you will find a nonfiction, fiction, poetry, and drama passage. **SKU:** 2054	$5.00
	Six Syllables Drama **SKU:** 8035	$10.00
	Sound Wall Activity Cards	An effective way to begin this important Science of Reading process in a systematic way. **SKU:** 2061	$15.00
	Sound Wall Bulletin Board Pieces	An effective way to begin this important Science of Reading process in a systematic way. **SKU:** 2081	$20.00

Sounds of -ed | This item is a one-page chart that explains the different ways to create the /ed/ sound. SKU: 2042		$0.00
The GAP Year Phonics Curriculum Grades 3-7 SKU: 9033		$75.00
The GAP Year Phonics Foundational Curriculum Grades PK-2 SKU: 9034		$75.00
Word Family Book - ag | This word family booklet emphasizes the word family - ag. It goes great in a station or as individual work sent home to further the home to school connection. SKU: 1011		$1.00
Word Family Book - am | This word family booklet emphasizes the word family - am. It goes great in a station or as individual work sent home to further the home to school connection. SKU: 1005		$1.00
Word Family Book - ame | This word family booklet emphasizes the word family - ame. It goes great in a station or as individual work sent home to further the home to school connection. SKU: 1004		$1.00
Word Family Book - ap | This word family booklet emphasizes the word family - ap. It goes great in a station or as individual work sent home to further the home to school connection. SKU: 1016		$1.00
Word Family Book - ool | This word family booklet emphasizes the word family - ool. It goes great in a station or as individual work sent home to further the home to school connection. SKU: 1060		$1.00
Word Family Book-oke | This word family booklet emphasizes the word family — oke. It goes great in a station or as individual work sent home to further the home to school connection. SKU: 1055		$1.00

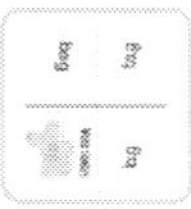

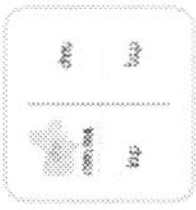

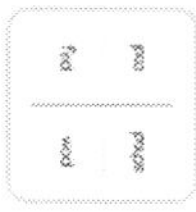

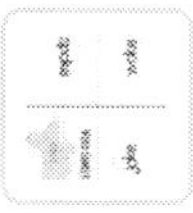

Word Family Books - eep. | This word family booklet emphasizes the word family — eep. It goes great in a station or as individual work sent home to further the home to school connection. $1.00

SKU: 1024

Word Family Books - ack | This word family booklet emphasizes the word family — ack. It goes great in a station or as individual work sent home to further the home to school connection. $1.00

SKU: 1013

Word Family Books - ad | This word family booklet emphasizes the word family — ad. It goes great in a station or as individual work sent home to further the home to school connection. $1.00

SKU: 1012

Word Family Books - age | This word family booklet emphasizes the word family — age. It goes great in a station or as individual work sent home to further the home to school connection. $1.00

SKU: 1010

Word Family Books - ail | This word family booklet emphasizes the word family — ail. It goes great in a station or as individual work sent home to further the home to school connection. $1.00

SKU: 1009

Word Family Books - ake | This word family booklet emphasizes the word family — ake. It goes great in a station or as individual work sent home to further the home to school connection. $1.00

SKU: 1007

Word Family Books - an | This word family booklet emphasizes the word family — an. It goes great in a station or as individual work sent home to further the home to school connection. $1.00

SKU: 1014

Word Family Books - ane | This word family booklet emphasizes the word family — ane. It goes great in a station or as individual work sent home to further the home to school connection. $1.00

SKU: 1008

Word Family Books - ank | This word family booklet emphasizes the word family — ank. It goes great in a station or as individual work sent home to further the home to school connection. $1.00

SKU: 1015

Word Family Books - ar | This word family booklet emphasizes the word family — ar. It goes great in a station or as individual work sent home to further the home to school connection.

SKU: 1017

$1.00

Word Family Books - ash | This word family booklet emphasizes the word family — ash. It goes great in a station or as individual work sent home to further the home to school connection.

SKU: 1018

$1.00

Word Family Books - at | This word family booklet emphasizes the word family — at. It goes great in a station or as individual work sent home to further the home to school connection.

SKU: 1019

$1.00

Word Family Books - ate | This word family booklet emphasizes the word family — ate. It goes great in a station or as individual work sent home to further the home to school connection.

SKU: 1020

$1.00

Word Family Books - aw | This word family booklet emphasizes the word family — aw. It goes great in a station or as individual work sent home to further the home to school connection.

SKU: 1021

$1.00

Word Family Books - eat | This word family booklet emphasizes the word family — eat. It goes great in a station or as individual work sent home to further the home to school connection.

SKU: 1022

$1.00

Word Family Books - eel | This word family booklet emphasizes the word family — eel. It goes great in a station or as individual work sent home to further the home to school connection.

SKU: 1023

$1.00

Word Family Books - eet | This word family booklet emphasizes the word family — eet. It goes great in a station or as individual work sent home to further the home to school connection.

SKU: 1025

$1.00

Word Family Books - ell | This word family booklet emphasizes the word family — ell. It goes great in a station or as individual work sent home to further the home to school connection.

SKU: 1026

$1.00

Word Family Books - en | This word family booklet emphasizes the word family — en. It goes great in a station or as individual work sent home to further the home to school connection.

SKU: 1028

$1.00

Word Family Books - ent | This word family booklet emphasizes the word family — ent. It goes great in a station or as individual work sent home to further the home to school connection.

SKU: 1029

$1.00

Word Family Books - est | This word family booklet emphasizes the word family — est. It goes great in a station or as individual work sent home to further the home to school connection.

SKU: 1027

$1.00

Word Family Books - ice | This word family booklet emphasizes the word family — ice. It goes great in a station or as individual work sent home to further the home to school connection.

SKU: 1030

$1.00

Word Family Books - ick | This word family booklet emphasizes the word family — ick. It goes great in a station or as individual work sent home to further the home to school connection.

SKU: 1031

$1.00

Word Family Books - ide | This word family booklet emphasizes the word family — ide. It goes great in a station or as individual work sent home to further the home to school connection.

SKU: 1032

$1.00

Word Family Books - ife | This word family booklet emphasizes the word family — ife. It goes great in a station or as individual work sent home to further the home to school connection.

SKU: 1033

$1.00

Word Family Books - ight | This word family booklet emphasizes the word family — ight. It goes great in a station or as individual work sent home to further the home to school connection.

SKU: 1034

$1.00

Word Family Books - ile | This word family booklet emphasizes the word family — ile. It goes great in a station or as individual work sent home to further the home to school connection.

SKU: 1035

$1.00

Word Family Books - ill | This word family booklet emphasizes the word family — ill. It goes great in a station or as individual work sent home to further the home to school connection.

SKU: 1036

$1.00

Word Family Books - in | This word family booklet emphasizes the word family — in. It goes great in a station or as individual work sent home to further the home to school connection.

SKU: 1040

$1.00

Word Family Books - ink | This word family booklet emphasizes the word family — ink. It goes great in a station or as individual work sent home to further the home to school connection.

SKU: 1039

$1.00

Word Family Books - ip | This word family booklet emphasizes the word family — ip. It goes great in a station or as individual work sent home to further the home to school connection.

SKU: 1041

$1.00

Word Family Books - it | This word family booklet emphasizes the word family — it. It goes great in a station or as individual work sent home to further the home to school connection.

SKU: 1042

$1.00

Word Family Books - oak | This word family booklet emphasizes the word family — oak. It goes great in a station or as individual work sent home to further the home to school connection.

SKU: 1043

$1.00

Word Family Books - ock | This word family booklet emphasizes the word family — ock. It goes great in a station or as individual work sent home to further the home to school connection.

SKU: 1044

$1.00

Word Family Books - oil | This word family booklet emphasizes the word family — oil. It goes great in a station or as individual work sent home to further the home to school connection.

SKU: 1048

$1.00

Word Family Books - on | This word family booklet emphasizes the word family — on. It goes great in a station or as individual work sent home to further the home to school connection.

SKU: 1061

$1.00

Word Family Books - one | This word family booklet emphasizes the word family — one. It goes great in a station or as individual work sent home to further the home to school connection. SKU: 1037		$1.00
Word Family Books - oo | This word family booklet emphasizes the word family — oo. It goes great in a station or as individual work sent home to further the home to school connection. SKU: 1056		$1.00
Word Family Books - ood (as in Good) | This word family booklet emphasizes the word family — ood (as in Good). It goes great in a station or as individual work sent home to further the home to school connection. SKU: 1045		$1.00
Word Family Books - ood (as in Mood) | This word family booklet emphasizes the word family — ood (as in Mood). It goes great in a station or as individual work sent home to further the home to school connection. SKU: 1047		$1.00
Word Family Books - oof | This word family booklet emphasizes the word family — oof. It goes great in a station or as individual work sent home to further the home to school connection. SKU: 1057		$1.00
Word Family Books - ook | This word family booklet emphasizes the word family — ook. It goes great in a station or as individual work sent home to further the home to school connection. SKU: 1058		$1.00
Word Family Books - oom | This word family booklet emphasizes the word family — oom. It goes great in a station or as individual work sent home to further the home to school connection. SKU: 1059		$1.00
Word Family Books - op | This word family booklet emphasizes the word family — op. It goes great in a station or as individual work sent home to further the home to school connection. SKU: 1062		$1.00
Word Family Books - ore | This word family booklet emphasizes the word family — ore. It goes great in a station or as individual work sent home to further the home to school connection. SKU: 1063		$1.00

Word Family Books - orn | This word family booklet emphasizes the word family — orn. It goes great in a station or as individual work sent home to further the home to school connection. $1.00

SKU: 1064

Word Family Books - ot | This word family booklet emphasizes the word family — ot. It goes great in a station or as individual work sent home to further the home to school connection. $1.00

SKU: 1065

Word Family Books - ought | This word family booklet emphasizes the word family — ought. It goes great in a station or as individual work sent home to further the home to school connection. $1.00

SKU: 1066

Word Family Books - ould | This word family booklet emphasizes the word family — ould. It goes great in a station or as individual work sent home to further the home to school connection. $1.00

SKU: 1067

Word Family Books - ouse | This word family booklet emphasizes the word family — ouse. It goes great in a station or as individual work sent home to further the home to school connection. $1.00

SKU: 1068

Word Family Books - out | This word family booklet emphasizes the word family — out. It goes great in a station or as individual work sent home to further the home to school connection. $1.00

SKU: 1069

Word Family Books - ow (as in Snow) | This word family booklet emphasizes the word family — ow (as in Snow). It goes great in a station or as individual work sent home to further the home to school connection. $1.00

SKU: 1046

Word Family Books - ow (like cow) | This word family booklet emphasizes the word family — ow (like cow). It goes great in a station or as individual work sent home to further the home to school connection. $1.00

SKU: 1070

Word Family Books - own | This word family booklet emphasizes the word family — own. It goes great in a station or as individual work sent home to further the home to school connection. $1.00

SKU: 1071

Word Family Books - uck | This word family booklet emphasizes the word family — uck. It goes great in a station or as individual work sent home to further the home to school connection.

SKU: 1072

$1.00

Word Family Books - ug | This word family booklet emphasizes the word family — ug. It goes great in a station or as individual work sent home to further the home to school connection.

SKU: 1073

$1.00

Word Family Books - ump | This word family booklet emphasizes the word family — ump. It goes great in a station or as individual work sent home to further the home to school connection.

SKU: 1074

$1.00

Word Family Books - un | This word family booklet emphasizes the word family — un. It goes great in a station or as individual work sent home to further the home to school connection.

SKU: 1075

$1.00

Word Family Books - unk | This word family booklet emphasizes the word family — unk. It goes great in a station or as individual work sent home to further the home to school connection.

SKU: 1076

$1.00

World Family Book - all | This word family booklet emphasizes the word family - all. It goes great in a station or as individual work sent home to further the home to school connection.

SKU: 1006

$1.00

PRACTICE PASSAGE PACKAGES

Practice Passage: Set 3- 10th Grade **SKU:** 6092	$15.00
Practice Passage : Set 3 - 6th Grade **SKU:** 6065	$15.00
Practice Passage: Set 5 - 3rd Grade **SKU:** 7002	$15.00
Practice Passage : Set 3- 9th Grade **SKU:** 6085	$15.00
Practice Passage : Set 3 - 8th Grade **SKU:** 6077	$15.00
Practice Passage set 3-7th Grade **SKU:** 6072	$15.00
Practice Passage : Set 3-5th Grade **SKU:** 5020	$15.00
Practice Passage : Set 3 -4th Grade **SKU:** 5007	$15.00
Practice Passage : Set 1 - 3rd Grade **SKU:** 4092	$15.00

PRACTICE PASSAGE PACKAGES - 3RD GRADE

	Practice Passage : Set 2 - 3rd Grade SKU: 4080	$15.00
	Practice Passage : Set 1- 3rd Grade SKU: 3030	$15.00
	Practice Passage : Set 1 - 3rd Grade	SPANISH SKU: 4069	$15.00
	Practice Passage : Set 5 - 3rd Grade-SPANISH SKU: 7007	$15.00
	Practice Passage: Set 5 - 3rd Grade SKU: 7002	$15.00
	Passage Practice: Set 4 - 3rd Grade SKU: 6006	$15.00
	Practice Passage : Set 1 - 3rd Grade SKU: 4092	$15.00
	Practice Passage : Set 1 - 3rd Grade-SPANISH SKU: 4090	$15.00
	Practice Passage : Set 2 - 3rd Grade	SPANISH SKU: 4081	$15.00

PRACTICE PASSAGE PACKAGES - 4TH GRADE

Practice Passage : Set 1 - 4th Grade $15.00
SKU: 3082

Practice Passage : Set 3 -4th Grade $15.00
SKU: 5007

Practice Passage : Set 1 - 4th Grade | SPANISH $15.00
SKU: 4070

PRACTICE PASSAGE PACKAGES - 5TH GRADE

Practice Passage : Set 1 - 5th Grade $15.00
SKU: 4023

Practice Passage : Set 3- 5th Grade-SPANISH $15.00
SKU: 6051

Practice Passage : Set 3-5th Grade $15.00
SKU: 5020

Practice Passage : Set 1 - 5th Grade | SPANISH $15.00
SKU: 4071

PRACTICE PASSAGE PACKAGES - 6TH GRADE

Practice Passage : Set 1 - 6th Grade $15.00
SKU: 4007

Practice Passage : Set 3 - 6th Grade $15.00
SKU: 6065

PRACTICE PASSAGE PACKAGES - 7TH GRADE

Practice Passage set 3-7th Grade $15.00
SKU: 6072

Practice Passage : Set 1 - 7th Grade $15.00
SKU: 4012

PRACTICE PASSAGE PACKAGES - 8TH GRADE

Practice Passage : Set 3 - 8th Grade $15.00
SKU: 6077

Practice Passage : Set 1 – 8th Grade $15.00
SKU: 4017

PRACTICE PASSAGE PACKAGES - 9TH GRADE

Practice Passage : Set 1 - 9th Grade — $15.00
SKU: 4082

Practice Passage :Fiction-9th Grade-The New Addition — $5.00
SKU: 6083

Practice Passage : Set 3- 9th Grade — $15.00
SKU: 6085

PRACTICE PASSAGE PACKAGES - 10TH GRADE

TEKS Tribune Tools : Editing & Revising - 5th Grade Edition — $7.00
SKU: 6089

Practice Passage : Set 1 – 10th Grade — $15.00
SKU: 4039

Practice Passage: Set 3- 10th Grade — $15.00
SKU: 6092

Make N Take Phonics Flyer — $0.00
SKU: 5082

PRACTICE PASSAGES - 3RD GRADE

Practice Passage : Set 2 - 3rd Grade — $15.00
SKU: 4080

Practice Passage : Set 7 - 3rd Grade — $15.00
SKU: 8010

Practice Passage: Fiction-3rd Grade-Andria — $5.00
SKU: 4085

Practice Passage : Poetry – 3rd Grade – Autumn's Poem — $5.00
SKU: 4076

Practice Passage : Set 1 - 3rd Grade | SPANISH — $15.00
SKU: 4069

Practice Passage : Fiction - 3rd Grade - William Shakespeare — $5.00
SKU: 3025

Passage Practice : Drama - 3rd Grade - Summer Troubles — $5.00
SKU: 3014

Practice Passage : Set 7 - 3rd Grade | SPANISH — $15.00
SKU: 8011

Passage Practice: Nonfiction - 3rd Grade - Hoover Dam | SPANISH — $5.00
SKU: 8009

	Passage Practice: Nonfiction - 3rd Grade - Hoover Dam SKU: 8008	$5.00
	Passage Practice: Nonfiction - 3rd Grade - History of the Panama Canal | SPANISH SKU: 8007	$5.00
	Passage Practice: Nonfiction - 3rd Grade - History of the Panama Canal SKU: 8006	$5.00
	Practice Passage : Nonfiction – 3rd Grade – The Cajun Navy | SPANISH SKU: 8005	$5.00
	Practice Passage : Nonfiction – 3rd Grade – The Cajun Navy SKU: 8004	$5.00
	Practice Passage : Drama – 3rd Grade – Garner State Park | SPANISH SKU: 8003	$5.00
	Practice Passage : Drama – 3rd Grade – Garner State Park SKU: 8002	$5.00
	Practice Passage :Non Fiction – 3rd Grade – The Author, the Hero-SPANISH SKU: 7006	$5.00
	Practice Passage: Non Fiction -3rd Grade-The Evolution of Wonder Woman-SPANISH SKU: 7005	$5.00
	Practice Passage : Non Fiction-3rd Grade-Spider Man-SPANISH SKU: 7004	$5.00
	Practice Passage: Non Fiction- 3rd Grade- Captain America Lives Through the Years-SPANISH SKU: 7003	$5.00

Practice Passage : Non Fiction 3rd Grade – The Author, the Hero SKU: 7000		$5.00
Practice Passage: Non Fiction-3rd Grade-The Evolution of Wonder Women SKU: 6097		$5.00
Practice Passage : Non Fiction – 3rd Grade – Spider Man SKU: 6094		$5.00
Practice Passage : Non Fiction – 3rd Grade – Captain America Lives Through the Years SKU: 6093		$5.00
Passage Practice: Nonfiction - 3rd Grade - How the Magic is Born	Spanish SKU: 6005		$5.00
Passage Practice: Nonfiction - 3rd Grade - How the Magic is Born SKU: 6004		$5.00
Passage Practice: Nonfiction - 3rd Grade - Benefits of Peppermint	SPANISH SKU: 6003		$5.00
Passage Practice: Nonfiction - 3rd Grade - Benefits of Peppermint SKU: 6002		$5.00
Passage Practice: Fiction - 3rd Grade - A Winter's Gift	SPANISH SKU: 6001		$5.00
Passage Practice: Fiction - 3rd Grade - A Winter's Gift SKU: 6000		$5.00
Passage Practice : Drama - 3rd Grade - Home for the Holidays	SPANISH SKU: 5099		$5.00

	Practice Passage : Drama – 3rd Grade – Home for the Holidays SKU: 5098	$5.00
	Practice Passage : Fiction – 3rd Grade – The New Addition-SPANISH SKU: 4089	$5.00
	TITLE : Practice Passage : Fiction – 3rd Grade – Andria-SPANISH SKU: 4088	$5.00
	Practice Passage : Drama – 3rd Grade –The Quarter-SPANISH SKU: 4087	$5.00
	Practice Passage: Non Fiction-3rd Grade-The History of Thanksgiving SKU: 4086	$5.00
	TITLE : Practice Passage : Drama – 3rd Grade – The Quarter SKU: 4084	$5.00
	Practice Passage : Set 2 - 3rd Grade	SPANISH SKU: 4081	$15.00
	Practice Passage : Nonfiction – 3rd Grade – Why Leaves Change Colors	SPANISH SKU: 4079	$5.00
	Practice Passage : Nonfiction – 3rd Grade – Why Leaves Change Colors SKU: 4078	$5.00
	Practice Passage : Poetry – 3rd Grade – Autumn's Poem	SPANISH SKU: 4077	$5.00
	Practice Passage : Nonfiction – 3rd Grade – Patrick Mahomes	SPANISH SKU: 4075	$5.00

Practice Passage : Nonfiction – 3rd Grade – Patrick Mahomes SKU: 4074		$5.00
Practice Passage : Nonfiction – 3rd Grade – The Invention of the Crayola | SPANISH SKU: 4073		$5.00
Practice Passage : Nonfiction – 3rd Grade – Invention of the Crayola SKU: 4072		$5.00
Practice Passage : Fiction - 3rd Grade - William Shakespeare | SPANISH SKU: 3027		$5.00
Practice Passage : Fiction - 3rd Grade - The Award | SPANISH SKU: 3017		$5.00
Practice Passage : Fiction - 3rd Grade - The Award SKU: 3016		$5.00
Passage Practice : Drama - 3rd Grade - Summer Troubles | SPANISH SKU: 3015		$5.00
Practice Passage : Nonfiction - 3rd Grade - Sam Walton-From the Great Depression to Billionaire | SPANISH SKU: 3022		$5.00
Practice Passage : Nonfiction - 3rd Grade - Sam Walton-From the Great Depression to Billionaire SKU: 3020		$5.00

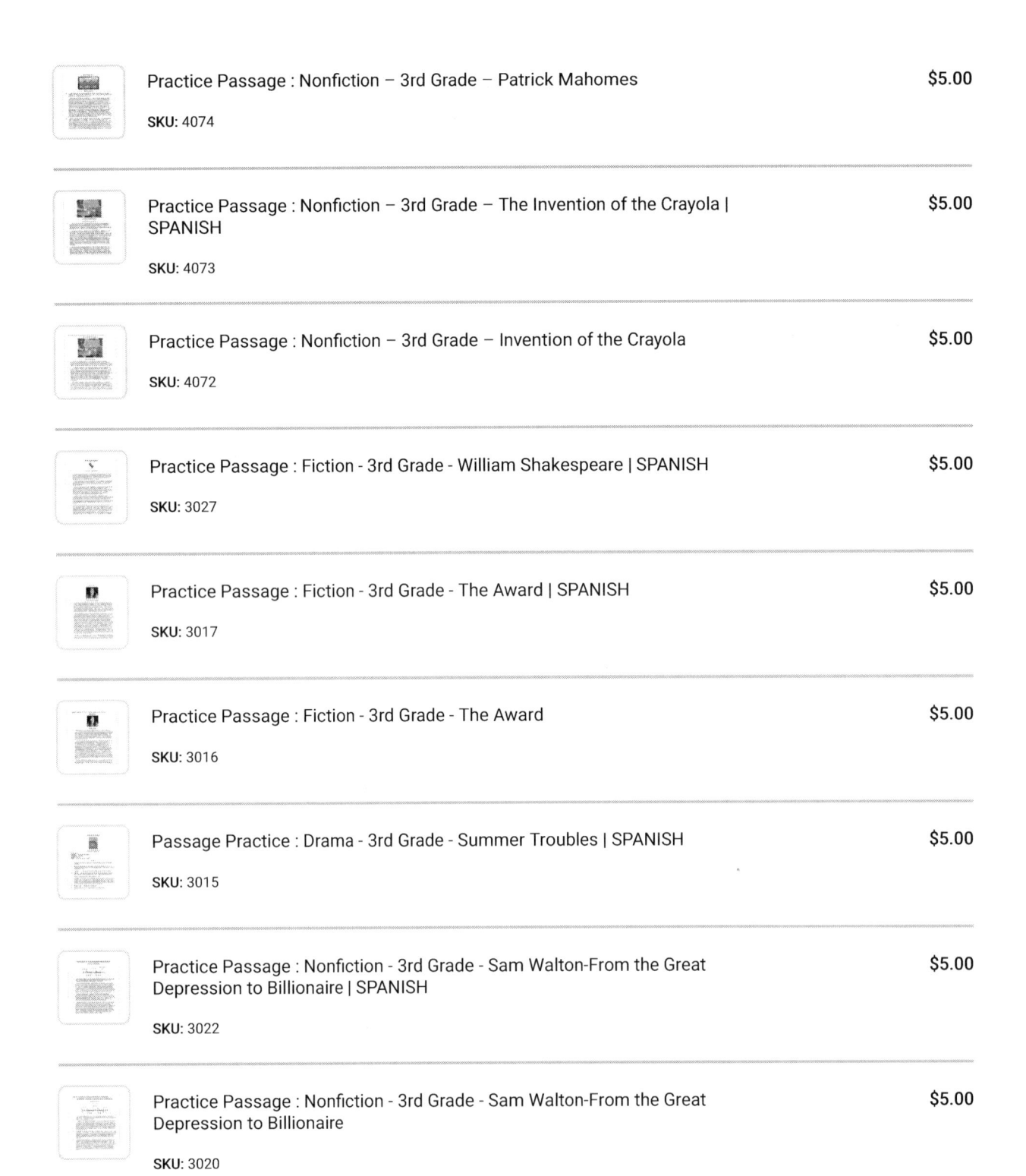

PRACTICE PASSAGES - 4TH GRADE

Passage Practice: Set 4 - 4th Grade **SKU:** 6015		$15.00
Practice Passage: Nonfiction-4th Grade- Sam Walton - From the Great Depression to Billionaire **SKU:** 3050		$5.00
Passage Practice: Set 7 - 4th Grade **SKU:** 8020		$15.00
Passage Practice: Nonfiction - 4th Grade - How the Magic is Born **SKU:** 6013		$5.00
Passage Practice: Drama - 4th Grade - Home for the Holidays **SKU:** 6007		$5.00
Practice Passage: Nonfiction 4th Grade- Sam Walton	SPANISH **SKU:** 3051		$5.00
Practice Passage: Fiction- 4th Grade- William Shakespeare	SPANISH **SKU:** 3054		$5.00
Practice Passage: Fiction – 4th Grade- The Award	SPANISH **SKU:** 3049		$5.00
Practice Passage: Drama-4th Grade- Summer Troubles	SPANISH **SKU:** 3047		$5.00

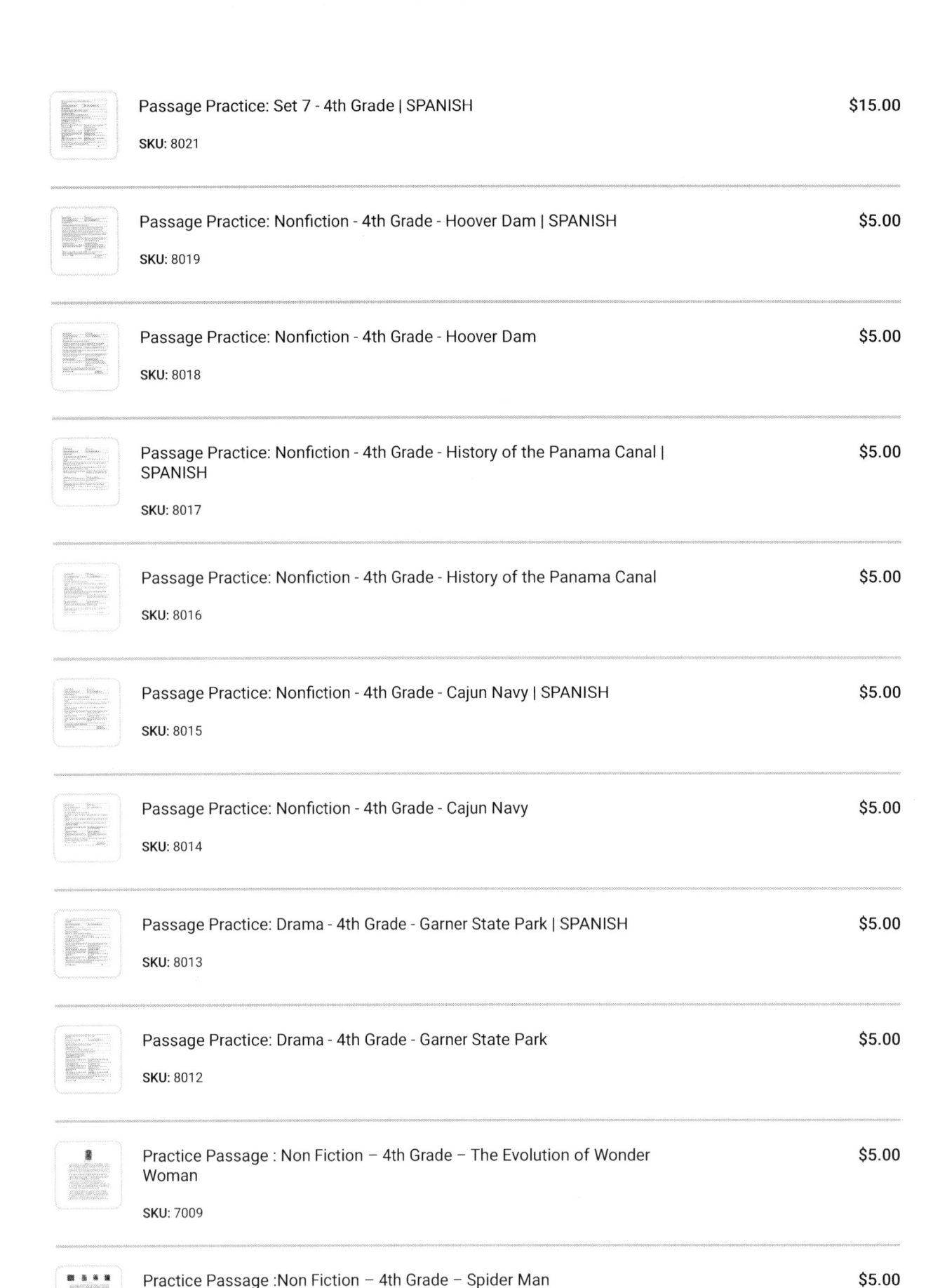

	Passage Practice: Set 7 - 4th Grade	SPANISH SKU: 8021	$15.00
	Passage Practice: Nonfiction - 4th Grade - Hoover Dam	SPANISH SKU: 8019	$5.00
	Passage Practice: Nonfiction - 4th Grade - Hoover Dam SKU: 8018	$5.00
	Passage Practice: Nonfiction - 4th Grade - History of the Panama Canal	SPANISH SKU: 8017	$5.00
	Passage Practice: Nonfiction - 4th Grade - History of the Panama Canal SKU: 8016	$5.00
	Passage Practice: Nonfiction - 4th Grade - Cajun Navy	SPANISH SKU: 8015	$5.00
	Passage Practice: Nonfiction - 4th Grade - Cajun Navy SKU: 8014	$5.00
	Passage Practice: Drama - 4th Grade - Garner State Park	SPANISH SKU: 8013	$5.00
	Passage Practice: Drama - 4th Grade - Garner State Park SKU: 8012	$5.00
	Practice Passage : Non Fiction – 4th Grade – The Evolution of Wonder Woman SKU: 7009	$5.00
	Practice Passage :Non Fiction – 4th Grade – Spider Man SKU: 7008	$5.00

	Passage Practice: Set 4 - 4th Grade | Spanish **SKU:** 6016	$15.00
	Passage Practice: Nonfiction - 4th Grade - How the Magic is Born | Spanish **SKU:** 6014	$5.00
	Passage Practice: Nonfiction - 4th Grade - Benefits of Peppermint | Spanish **SKU:** 6012	$5.00
	Passage Practice: Nonfiction - 4th Grade - Benefits of Peppermint **SKU:** 6011	$5.00
	Passage Practice: Fiction - 4th Grade - A Winter's Gift | Spanish **SKU:** 6010	$5.00
	Passage Practice: Fiction - 4th Grade - A Winter's Gift **SKU:** 6009	$5.00
	Passage Practice: Drama - 4th Grade - Home for the Holidays | Spanish **SKU:** 6008	$5.00
	Practice Passage : Set 3 - 4th Grade-SPANISH **SKU:** 5008	$15.00
	Practice Passage : Non Fiction – 4th Grade – The History of Thanksgiving-SPANISH **SKU:** 5006	$5.00
	Practice Passage : Non Fiction – 4th Grade – The History of Thanksgiving **SKU:** 5005	$5.00
	Practice Passage : Fiction – 4th Grade –The New Addition **SKU:** 4098	$5.00

	Practice Passage : Fiction – 4th Grade – Andria-SPANISH SKU: 4097	$5.00
	Practice Passage : Fiction – 4th Grade – Andria SKU: 4096	$5.00
	Practice Passage : Drama – 4th Grade –The Quarter-SPANISH SKU: 4094	$5.00
	Practice Passage : Drama – 4th Grade – The Quarter SKU: 4093	$5.00
	Practice Passage : Set 1 - 4th Grade | SPANISH SKU: 4070	$15.00
	Practice Passage: Fiction – 4th Grade- William Shakespeare SKU: 3052	$5.00
	Practice Passage: Fiction – 4th Grade- The Award SKU: 3048	$5.00
	Practice Passage: Drama - 4th Grade - Summer Troubles SKU: 3045	$5.00

PRACTICE PASSAGES - 5TH GRADE

	Passage Practice: Set 7 - 5th Grade **SKU:** 8030	$15.00
	Passage Practice: Nonfiction - 5th Grade - The Cajun Navy	SPANISH **SKU:** 8029	$5.00
	Passage Practice: Set 4 - 5th Grade **SKU:** 6025	$15.00
	Practice Passage : Fiction – 5th Grade – The New Addition **SKU:** 5016	$5.00
	Passage Practice: Nonfiction - 5th Grade - The Cajun Navy **SKU:** 8028	$5.00
	Passage Practice: Nonfiction - 5th Grade - Hoover Dam	SPANISH **SKU:** 8027	$5.00
	Passage Practice: Nonfiction - 5th Grade - Hoover Dam **SKU:** 8026	$5.00
	Passage Practice: Nonfiction - 5th Grade - History of the Panama Canal	SPANISH **SKU:** 8025	$5.00
	Passage Practice: Nonfiction - 5th Grade - History of the Panama Canal **SKU:** 8024	$5.00

Passage Practice: Drama - 5th Grade - Garner State Park | SPANISH SKU: 8023		$5.00
Passage Practice: Drama - 5th Grade - Garner State Park SKU: 8022		$5.00
Passage Practice: Set 4 - 5th Grade | Spanish SKU: 6026		$15.00
Passage Practice: Nonfiction - 5th Grade - How the Magic is Born | Spanish SKU: 6024		$5.00
Passage Practice: Nonfiction - 5th Grade - How the Magic is Born SKU: 6023		$5.00
Passage Practice: Nonfiction - 5th Grade - Benefits of Peppermint | Spanish SKU: 6022		$5.00
Passage Practice: Nonfiction - 5th Grade - Benefits of Peppermint SKU: 6021		$5.00
Passage Practice: Fiction - 5th Grade - A Winter's Gift | Spanish SKU: 6020		$5.00
Passage Practice: Fiction - 5th Grade - A Winter's Gift SKU: 6019		$5.00
Passage Practice: Drama - 5th Grade - Home for the Holidays | Spanish SKU: 6018		$5.00
Passage Practice: Drama - 5th Grade - Home for the Holidays SKU: 6017		$5.00

	Practice Passage :Non Fiction – 5th Grade – The History of Thanksgiving-SPANISH **SKU:** 5019	$5.00
	Practice Passage : Non Fiction – 5th Grade – The History of Thanksgiving **SKU:** 5018	$5.00
	Practice Passage : Fiction – 5th Grade – The New Addition-SPANISH **SKU:** 5017	$5.00
	Practice Passage : Fiction – 5th Grade – Andria-SPANISH **SKU:** 5015	$5.00
	Practice Passage : Fiction – 5th Grade – Andria **SKU:** 5014	$5.00
	Practice Passage : Drama – 5th Grade – The Quarter-SPANISH **SKU:** 5013	$5.00
	Practice Passage : Drama – 5th Grade – The Quarter **SKU:** 5012	$5.00
	Practice Passage : Set 1 - 5th Grade	SPANISH **SKU:** 4071	$15.00
	Practice Passage : Fiction - 5th Grade - William Shakespeare	SPANISH **SKU:** 4022	$5.00
	Practice Passage : Fiction - 5th Grade - William Shakespeare **SKU:** 4021	$5.00
	Practice Passage : Nonfiction - 5th Grade - Sam Walton - From the Great Depression to Billionaire	SPANISH **SKU:** 4020	$5.00

	Practice Passage : Nonfiction – 5th Grade – Sam Walton - From the Great Depression to Billionaire **SKU:** 4019	$5.00
	Practice Passage : Fiction - 5th Grade - The Award | SPANISH **SKU:** 4018	$5.00
	Practice Passage : Fiction – 5th Grade – The Award **SKU:** 3081	$5.00
	Practice Passage : Drama – 5th Grade – Summer Troubles | SPANISH **SKU:** 3080	$5.00
	Practice Passage : Drama - 5th Grade - Summer Troubles **SKU:** 3079	$5.00

PRACTICE PASSAGES - 6TH GRADE

Practice Passage :Non Fiction – 6th Grade – The Cajun Navy **SKU:** 4005		$5.00
Practice Passage: Non Fiction-6th Grade -The History of Thanksgiving **SKU:** 6055		$5.00
Practice Passage: Fiction-6th Grade-The New Addition **SKU:** 6054		$5.00
Practice Passage : Fiction – 6th Grade – Andria **SKU:** 6053		$5.00
Practice Passage : Drama – 6th Grade – The Quarter **SKU:** 6052		$5.00
Passage Practice: Set 4 - 6th Grade **SKU:** 6030		$15.00
Passage Practice: Nonfiction - 6th Grade - Benefits of Peppermint **SKU:** 6029		$5.00
Passage Practice: Fiction - 6th Grade - A Winter's Gift **SKU:** 6028		$5.00
Passage Practice: Drama - 6th Grade - Home for the Holidays **SKU:** 6027		$5.00

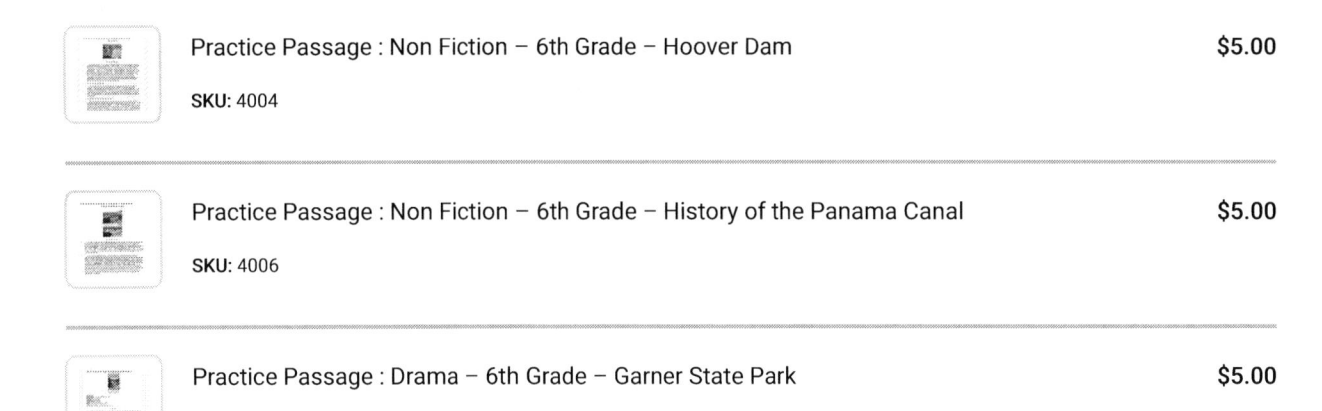

Practice Passage : Non Fiction – 6th Grade – Hoover Dam	$5.00
SKU: 4004	

Practice Passage : Non Fiction – 6th Grade – History of the Panama Canal	$5.00
SKU: 4006	

Practice Passage : Drama – 6th Grade – Garner State Park	$5.00
SKU: 4003	

PRACTICE PASSAGES - 7TH GRADE

Practice Passage : Non Fiction – 7th Grade – The Cajun Navy SKU: 4011		$5.00
Practice Passage: Non Fiction-7th Grade-The History of Thanksgiving SKU: 6071		$5.00
Practice Passage:Fiction-7th Grade-The New Addition SKU: 6070		$5.00
Practice Passage: Fiction- 7th grade-Andria SKU: 6069		$5.00
Practice Passage: Drama-7th Grade-The Quarter SKU: 6068		$5.00
Passage Practice: Set 4 - 7th Grade SKU: 6035		$15.00
Passage Practice: Nonfiction - 7th Grade - How the Magic is Born SKU: 6034		$5.00
Passage Practice: Nonfiction - 7th Grade - Benefits of Peppermint SKU: 6033		$5.00
Passage Practice: Fiction - 7th Grade - A Winter's Gift SKU: 6032		$5.00

Passage Practice: Drama - 7th Grade - Home for the Holidays **SKU:** 6031		$5.00
Practice Passage :Non Fiction – 7th Grade – Hoover Dam **SKU:** 4010		$5.00
Practice Passage : Non Fiction – 7th Grade – History of the Panama Canal **SKU:** 4009		$5.00
Practice Passage : Drama – 7th Grade – Garner State Park **SKU:** 4008		$5.00

PRACTICE PASSAGES - 8TH GRADE

	Practice Passage : Drama – 8th Grade – Garner State Park **SKU:** 4013	$5.00
	Practice Passage :Non Fiction – 8th Grade –The History of Thanksgiving **SKU:** 6076	$5.00
	Practice Passage :Fiction – 8th Grade – The New Addition **SKU:** 6075	$5.00
	Practice Passage : Fiction– 8th Grade – Andria **SKU:** 6074	$5.00
	Practice Passage : Drama – 8th Grade – The Quarter **SKU:** 6073	$5.00
	Passage Practice: Set 4 - 8th Grade **SKU:** 6040	$15.00
	Passage Practice: Nonfiction - 8th Grade - How the Magic is Born **SKU:** 6039	$5.00
	Passage Practice: Nonfiction - 8th Grade - Benefits of Peppermint **SKU:** 6038	$5.00
	Passage Practice: Fiction - 8th Grade - A Winter's Gift **SKU:** 6037	$5.00

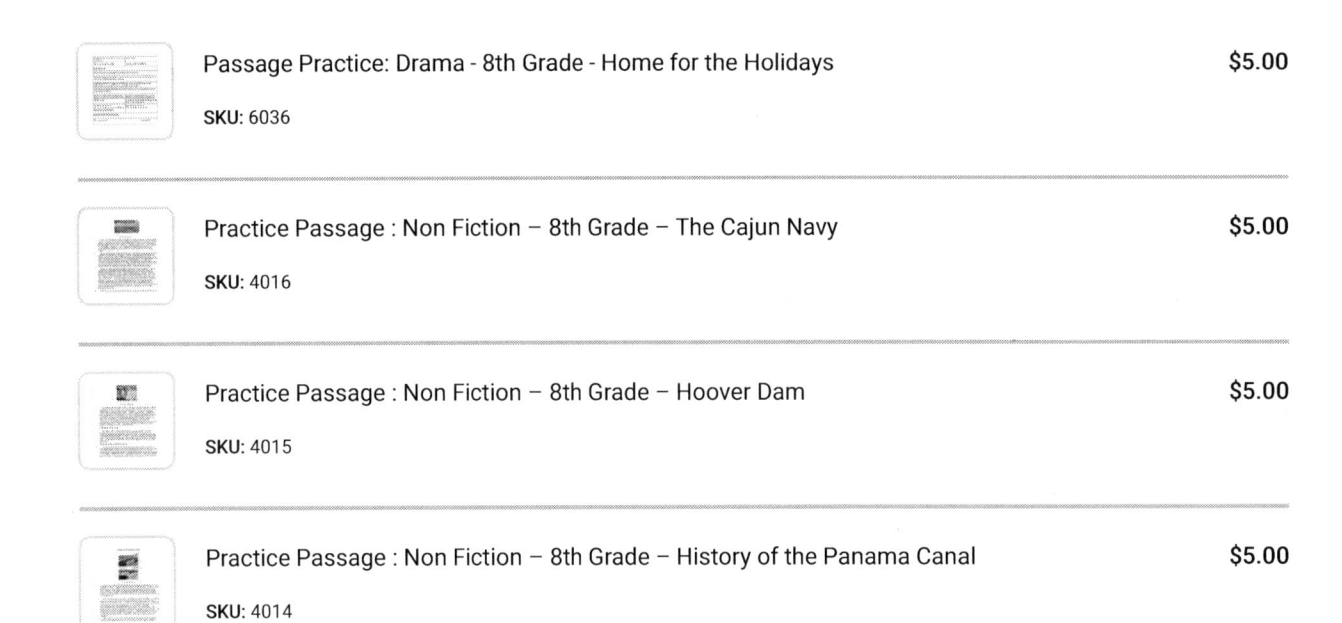

Passage Practice: Drama - 8th Grade - Home for the Holidays	$5.00
SKU: 6036	
Practice Passage : Non Fiction – 8th Grade – The Cajun Navy	$5.00
SKU: 4016	
Practice Passage : Non Fiction – 8th Grade – Hoover Dam	$5.00
SKU: 4015	
Practice Passage : Non Fiction – 8th Grade – History of the Panama Canal	$5.00
SKU: 4014	

PRACTICE PASSAGES - 9TH GRADE

Practice Passage:Non Fiction - 9th Grade-The History of Thanksgiving SKU: 6084	$5.00
Practice Passage : Fiction – 9th Grade – Andria SKU: 6082	$5.00
Practice Passage : Drama – 9th Grade – The Quarter SKU: 6081	$5.00
Practice Passage : Drama – 9th Grade – Garner State Park SKU: 4031	$5.00
Passage Practice: Set 4 - 9th Grade SKU: 6045	$15.00
Passage Practice: Nonfiction - 9th Grade - How the Magic is Born SKU: 6044	$5.00
Passage Practice: Nonfiction - 9th Grade - Benefits of Peppermint SKU: 6043	$5.00
Passage Practice: Fiction - 9th Grade - A Winter's Gift SKU: 6042	$5.00
Passage Practice: Drama - 9th Grade - Home for the Holidays SKU: 6041	$5.00

Practice Passage : Non Fiction – 9th Grade – The Cajun Navy SKU: 4034		$5.00
Practice Passage : Non Fiction – 9th Grade – Hoover Dam SKU: 4033		$5.00
Practice Passage :Non Fiction – 9th Grade – History of the Panama Canal SKU: 4032		$5.00

PRACTICE PASSAGES - 10TH GRADE

Practice Passage : Drama – 10th Grade – Garner State Park SKU: 4035		$5.00
Passage Practice: Nonfiction - 10th Grade - Benefits of Peppermint SKU: 6048		$5.00
Passage Practice: Fiction - 10th Grade - A Winter's Gift SKU: 6047		$5.00
Passage Practice: Drama - 10th Grade - Home for the Holidays SKU: 6046		$5.00
Practice Passage : Non Fiction – 10th Grade – History of the Panama Canal SKU: 4036		$5.00
Practice Passage : Non Fiction-10th Grade-The History of Thanksgiving SKU: 6091		$5.00
Practice Passage : Fiction -10th Grade-The New Addition SKU: 6090		$5.00
Practice Passage : Fiction-10th Grade-Andria SKU: 6087		$5.00
Practice Passage : Drama -10th Grade-The Quarter SKU: 6086		$5.00

Passage Practice: Set 4 - 10th Grade **SKU:** 6050		$15.00
Passage Practice: Nonfiction - 10th Grade - How the Magic Begins **SKU:** 6049		$5.00
Practice Passage : Non Fiction – 10th Grade – The Cajun Navy **SKU:** 4038		$5.00
Practice Passage : Non Fiction – 10th Grade – Hoover Dam **SKU:** 4037		$5.00

READING COMPREHENSION

A Time and Place for TRACKS	Think of this game as Candyland with a twist! Students will practice analyzing a text by looking for TRACKS. They will also practice using textual evidence to make inferences and identify thesis/claim of a passage. SKU: 3062	$1.00

Analyzing Theme | Students will practice analyzing textual evidence of paired passages.

SKU: 6064 — $4.00

Attention to Comprehension

SKU: 9035 — $12.00

Fluency Flows

SKU: 9042 — $12.00

Look It Up!

SKU: 9041 — $12.00

Paired Passages | With this item, students will practice analyzing textual evidence of paired passages.

SKU: 3012 — $5.00

Paragraph Power - Science - "Chickens" | Whether it is a small group, a paired student activity, or an independent reading comprehension activity that you are looking for, Paragraph Power has it all.

SKU: 2062 — $2.00

Paragraph Power - Science - "Cows" | Whether it is a small group, a paired student activity, or an independent reading comprehension activity that you are looking for, Paragraph Power has it all.

SKU: 2063 — $2.00

Paragraph Power - Science - "Life Cycle of Butterflies"	Whether it is a small group, a paired student activity, or an independent reading comprehension activity that you are looking for, Paragraph Power has it all. **SKU:** 2067	$2.00
Paragraph Power - Science - "Life Cycle of Frogs"	Whether it is a small group, a paired student activity, or an independent reading comprehension activity that you are looking for, Paragraph Power has it all. **SKU:** 2068	$2.00
Paragraph Power - Science - "Nests"	Whether it is a small group, a paired student activity, or an independent reading comprehension activity that you are looking for, Paragraph Power has it all. **SKU:** 2064	$2.00
Paragraph Power - Science - "Pigs"	Whether it is a small group, a paired student activity, or an independent reading comprehension activity that you are looking for, Paragraph Power has it all. **SKU:** 2065	$2.00
Paragraph Power - Science - "Trees"	Whether it is a small group, a paired student activity, or an independent reading comprehension activity that you are looking for, Paragraph Power has it all. **SKU:** 2069	$2.00
Paragraph Power - Social Studies - "Blue Bonnets"	Whether it is a small group, a paired student activity, or an independent reading comprehension activity that you are looking for, Paragraph Power has it all. **SKU:** 2073	$2.00
Paragraph Power - Social Studies - "Collecting Coins"	Whether it is a small group, a paired student activity, or an independent reading comprehension activity that you are looking for, Paragraph Power has it all. **SKU:** 2074	$2.00
Paragraph Power - Social Studies - "Community Helpers"	Whether it is a small group, a paired student activity, or an independent reading comprehension activity that you are looking for, Paragraph Power has it all. **SKU:** 2070	$2.00
Paragraph Power - Social Studies - "Family Traditions"	Whether it is a small group, a paired student activity, or an independent reading comprehension activity that you are looking for, Paragraph Power has it all. **SKU:** 2075	$2.00

| Paragraph Power - Social Studies - "Importance of Farming" | Whether it is a small group, a paired student activity, or an independent reading comprehension activity that you are looking for, Paragraph Power has it all.

SKU: 2076 | $2.00 |

Paragraph Power - Social Studies - "Importance of Maps" | Whether it is a small group, a paired student activity, or an independent reading comprehension activity that you are looking for, Paragraph Power has it all.

SKU: 2077 — $2.00

Paragraph Power - Social Studies - "Instruments" | Whether it is a small group, a paired student activity, or an independent reading comprehension activity that you are looking for, Paragraph Power has it all.

SKU: 2078 — $2.00

Paragraph Power - Social Studies - "Invention of Lamps" | Whether it is a small group, a paired student activity, or an independent reading comprehension activity that you are looking for, Paragraph Power has it all.

SKU: 2079 — $2.00

Paragraph Power - Social Studies - "July 4th" | Whether it is a small group, a paired student activity, or an independent reading comprehension activity that you are looking for, Paragraph Power has it all.

SKU: 2080 — $2.00

Paragraph Power - Social Studies - "Texas Flag" | Whether it is a small group, a paired student activity, or an independent reading comprehension activity that you are looking for, Paragraph Power has it all.

SKU: 2071 — $2.00

Paragraph Power - Social Studies - "Transportation" | Whether it is a small group, a paired student activity, or an independent reading comprehension activity that you are looking for, Paragraph Power has it all.

SKU: 2072 — $2.00

Question Stem Synonym Booklets

SKU: 3053 — $8.00

Selection Collection - Science - "Pigs" | Included in the Selection Collection, you will find a nonfiction, fiction, poetry, and drama passage.

SKU: 2057 — $5.00

Selection Collection - Science - "Spiders"	Included in the Selection Collection, you will find a nonfiction, fiction, poetry, and drama passage. SKU: 2056		$5.00
Selection Collection - Social Studies - "Blue Bonnet"	Included in the Selection Collection, you will find a nonfiction, fiction, poetry, and drama passage. SKU: 2053		$5.00
Selection Collection - Social Studies - "Collecting Coins"	Included in the Selection Collection, you will find a nonfiction, fiction, poetry, and drama passage. SKU: 2051		$5.00
Selection Collection - Social Studies - "Invention of Toilet Paper"	Included in the Selection Collection, you will find a nonfiction, fiction, poetry, and drama passage. SKU: 2050		$5.00
Selection Collection - Social Studies - "Johnny Appleseed"	Included in the Selection Collection, you will find a nonfiction, fiction, poetry, and drama passage. SKU: 2055		$5.00
Selection Collection - Social Studies - "Texas Flag"	Included in the Selection Collection, you will find a nonfiction, fiction, poetry, and drama passage. SKU: 2052		$5.00
Selection Collection - Social Studies - "Transportation"	Included in the Selection Collection, you will find a nonfiction, fiction, poetry, and drama passage. SKU: 2054		$5.00
Six Syllables Drama SKU: 8035		$10.00
Teaching Central Idea SKU: 2096		$5.00

Teaching Summary	The activities in this summary file will put an end to the exhaustion of answering summary questions by giving students the tools they need to identify the best summary of any paragraph or passage. SKU: 3013	$5.00
TRACKS	The parts of a passage and the secrets of a source SKU: 4030	$2.00
What Happened Next? SKU: 9044	$12.00

SELECTION COLLECTION - SCIENCE

Selection Collection - Science - Life Cycle of a Frog | Included in the Selection Collection, you will find a nonfiction, fiction, poetry, and drama passage.

SKU: 3084

$5.00

Selection Collection - Science - Astronomy & Stars | Included in the Selection Collection, you will find a nonfiction, fiction, poetry, and drama passage.

SKU: 3092

$5.00

Selection Collection - Science - Construction | Included in the Selection Collection, you will find a nonfiction, fiction, poetry, and drama passage.

SKU: 4000

$5.00

Selection Collection - Science - Gravity | Included in the Selection Collection, you will find a nonfiction, fiction, poetry, and drama passage.

SKU: 4002

$5.00

Selection Collection - Science - Habitats | Included in the Selection Collection, you will find a nonfiction, fiction, poetry, and drama passage.

SKU: 3097

$5.00

Selection Collection - Science - How Horses Communicate | Included in the Selection Collection, you will find a nonfiction, fiction, poetry, and drama passage.

SKU: 3086

$5.00

Selection Collection - Science - Instruments | Included in the Selection Collection, you will find a nonfiction, fiction, poetry, and drama passage.

SKU: 3095

$5.00

Selection Collection - Science - Magnets | Included in the Selection Collection, you will find a nonfiction, fiction, poetry, and drama passage.

SKU: 3098

$5.00

Selection Collection - Science - Mircroscopes	Included in the Selection Collection, you will find a nonfiction, fiction, poetry, and drama passage **SKU:** 3087	$5.00
Selection Collection - Science - Moon Phases	Included in the Selection Collection, you will find a nonfiction, fiction, poetry, and drama passage. **SKU:** 3089	$5.00
Selection Collection - Science - Seeds To Trees	Included in the Selection Collection, you will find a nonfiction, fiction, poetry, and drama passage. **SKU:** 3091	$5.00
Selection Collection - Science - Sink or Float	Included in the Selection Collection, you will find a nonfiction, fiction, poetry, and drama passage. **SKU:** 3096	$5.00
Selection Collection - Science - States of Matter	Included in the Selection Collection, you will find a nonfiction, fiction, poetry, and drama passage. **SKU:** 3099	$5.00
Selection Collection - Science - Surprising Things About Pigs	Included in the Selection Collection, you will find a nonfiction, fiction, poetry, and drama passage **SKU:** 3085	$5.00
Selection Collection - Science - Telescopes	Included in the Selection Collection, you will find a nonfiction, fiction, poetry, and drama passage. **SKU:** 3094	$5.00
Selection Collection - Science - Vibrations	Included in the Selection Collection, you will find a nonfiction, fiction, poetry, and drama passage. **SKU:** 4001	$5.00
Selection Collection - Science - Water Cycle	Included in the Selection Collection, you will find a nonfiction, fiction, poetry, and drama passage. **SKU:** 3093	$5.00
Selection Collection - Science - Weather	Included in the Selection Collection, you will find a nonfiction, fiction, poetry, and drama passage. **SKU:** 3090	$5.00

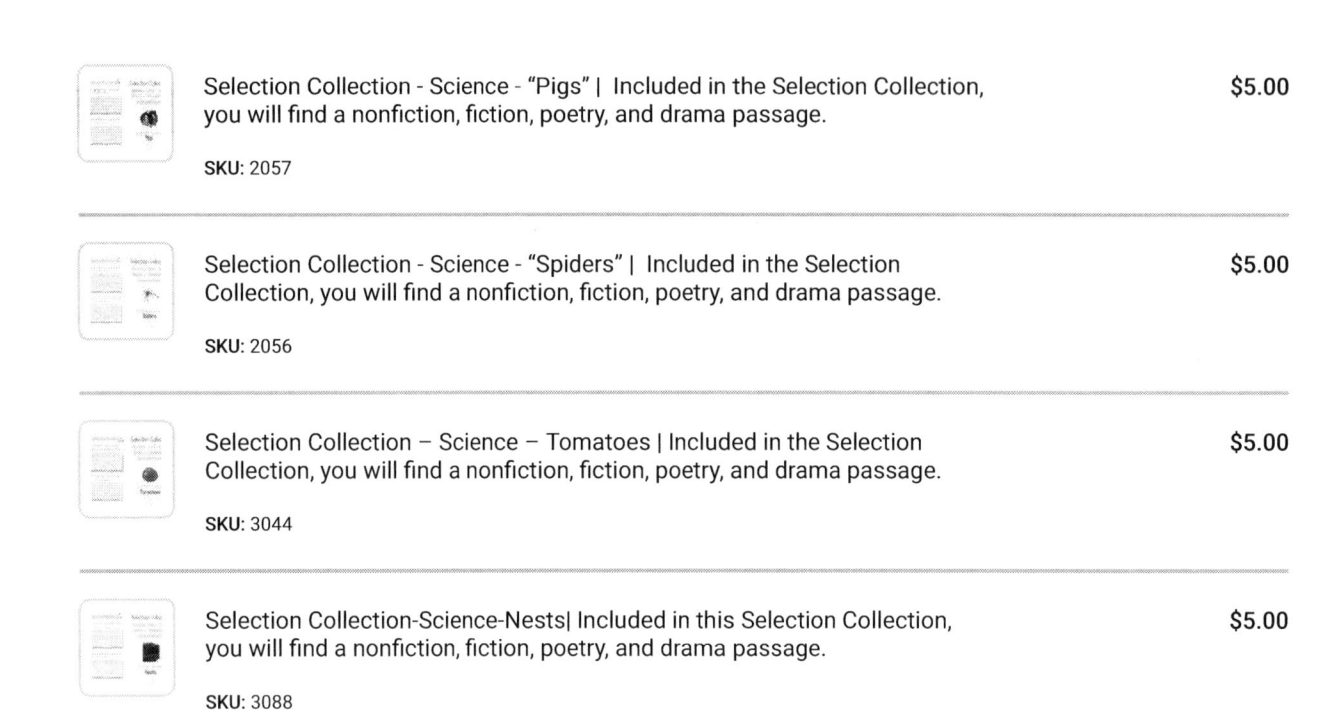

Selection Collection - Science - "Pigs"	Included in the Selection Collection, you will find a nonfiction, fiction, poetry, and drama passage. SKU: 2057	$5.00
Selection Collection - Science - "Spiders"	Included in the Selection Collection, you will find a nonfiction, fiction, poetry, and drama passage. SKU: 2056	$5.00
Selection Collection – Science – Tomatoes	Included in the Selection Collection, you will find a nonfiction, fiction, poetry, and drama passage. SKU: 3044	$5.00
Selection Collection-Science-Nests	Included in this Selection Collection, you will find a nonfiction, fiction, poetry, and drama passage. SKU: 3088	$5.00

SELECTION COLLECTION - SCIENCE - BUNDLES

Selection Collection Science - Bundle 1	Included in the Selection Collection, you will find a nonfiction, fiction, poetry, and drama passage. SKU: 2060	$15.00
Selection Collection Science - Bundle 4	Included in the Selection Collection, you will find a nonfiction, fiction, poetry, and drama passage. SKU: 4055	$15.00
Selection Collection Science - Bundle 3	Included in the Selection Collection, you will find a nonfiction, fiction, poetry, and drama passage. SKU: 4053	$15.00
Selection Collection Science - Bundle 2	Included in the Selection Collection, you will find a nonfiction, fiction, poetry, and drama passage. SKU: 4052	$15.00

SELECTION COLLECTION - SOCIAL STUDIES

Selection Collection - Social Studies - "Blue Bonnet" | Included in the Selection Collection, you will find a nonfiction, fiction, poetry, and drama passage. $5.00

SKU: 2053

Selection Collection - Social Studies - "Collecting Coins" | Included in the Selection Collection, you will find a nonfiction, fiction, poetry, and drama passage. $5.00

SKU: 2051

Selection Collection - Social Studies - "Invention of Toilet Paper" | Included in the Selection Collection, you will find a nonfiction, fiction, poetry, and drama passage. $5.00

SKU: 2050

Selection Collection - Social Studies - "Johnny Appleseed" | Included in the Selection Collection, you will find a nonfiction, fiction, poetry, and drama passage. $5.00

SKU: 2055

Selection Collection - Social Studies - "Texas Flag" | Included in the Selection Collection, you will find a nonfiction, fiction, poetry, and drama passage. $5.00

SKU: 2052

Selection Collection - Social Studies - "Transportation" | Included in the Selection Collection, you will find a nonfiction, fiction, poetry, and drama passage. $5.00

SKU: 2054

Selection Collection – Social Studies - Christopher Columbus | Included in the Selection Collection, you will find a nonfiction, fiction, poetry, and drama passage. $5.00

SKU: 3033

Selection Collection – Social Studies – July 4th	Included in the Selection Collection, you will find a nonfiction, fiction, poetry, and drama passage. **SKU:** 2094	$5.00
Selection Collection – Social Studies – Abraham Lincoln	Included in the Selection Collection, you will find a nonfiction, fiction, poetry, and drama passage. **SKU:** 2089	$5.00
Selection Collection – Social Studies – Alexander Graham Bell	Included in the Selection Collection, you will find a nonfiction, fiction, poetry, and drama passage. **SKU:** 2093	$5.00
Selection Collection – Social Studies – Community Helpers	Included in the Selection Collection, you will find a nonfiction, fiction, poetry, and drama passage. **SKU:** 3039	$5.00
Selection Collection – Social Studies – Eagle	Included in the Selection Collection, you will find a nonfiction, fiction, poetry, and drama passage. **SKU:** 2090	$5.00
Selection Collection – Social Studies – Henry Ford	Included in the Selection Collection, you will find a nonfiction, fiction, poetry, and drama passage. **SKU:** 3024	$5.00
Selection Collection – Social Studies – How Maps Help Us	Included in the Selection Collection, you will find a nonfiction, fiction, poetry, and drama passage. **SKU:** 3019	$5.00
Selection Collection – Social Studies – How To Be A Good Citizen	Included in the Selection Collection, you will find a nonfiction, fiction, poetry, and drama passage. **SKU:** 3023	$5.00
Selection Collection – Social Studies – Importance Of Laws	Included in the Selection Collection, you will find a nonfiction, fiction, poetry, and drama passage. **SKU:** 3037	$5.00

Selection Collection – Social Studies – Jose' Antonio Navarro	Included in the Selection Collection, you will find a nonfiction, fiction, poetry, and drama passage. **SKU:** 3034	$5.00
Selection Collection – Social Studies – Ronald Reagan	Included in the Selection Collection, you will find a nonfiction, fiction, poetry, and drama passage. **SKU:** 3036	$5.00
Selection Collection – Social Studies – Star Spangled Banner		Included in the Selection Collection, you will find a nonfiction, fiction, poetry, and drama passage. **SKU:** 3029	$5.00
Selection Collection – Social Studies – The American Flag	Included in the Selection Collection, you will find a nonfiction, fiction, poetry, and drama passage. **SKU:** 2092	$5.00
Selection Collection – Social Studies – The Importance of Family Traditions	Included in the Selection Collection, you will find a nonfiction, fiction, poetry, and drama passage. **SKU:** 3018	$5.00
Selection Collection – Social Studies – The Importance of Farming	Included in the Selection Collection, you will find a nonfiction, fiction, poetry, and drama passage. **SKU:** 3031	$5.00
Selection Collection – Social Studies – Value of Work	Included in the Selection Collection, you will find a nonfiction, fiction, poetry, and drama passage. **SKU:** 2099	$5.00
Selection Collection- Social Studies - "Sam Houston"	Included in the Selection Collection, you will find a nonfiction, fiction, poetry, and drama passage. **SKU:** 2088	$5.00
Selection Collection- Social Studies- Benjamin franklin	Included in the Selection Collection, you will find a nonfiction, fiction, poetry, and drama passage. **SKU:** 3035	$5.00

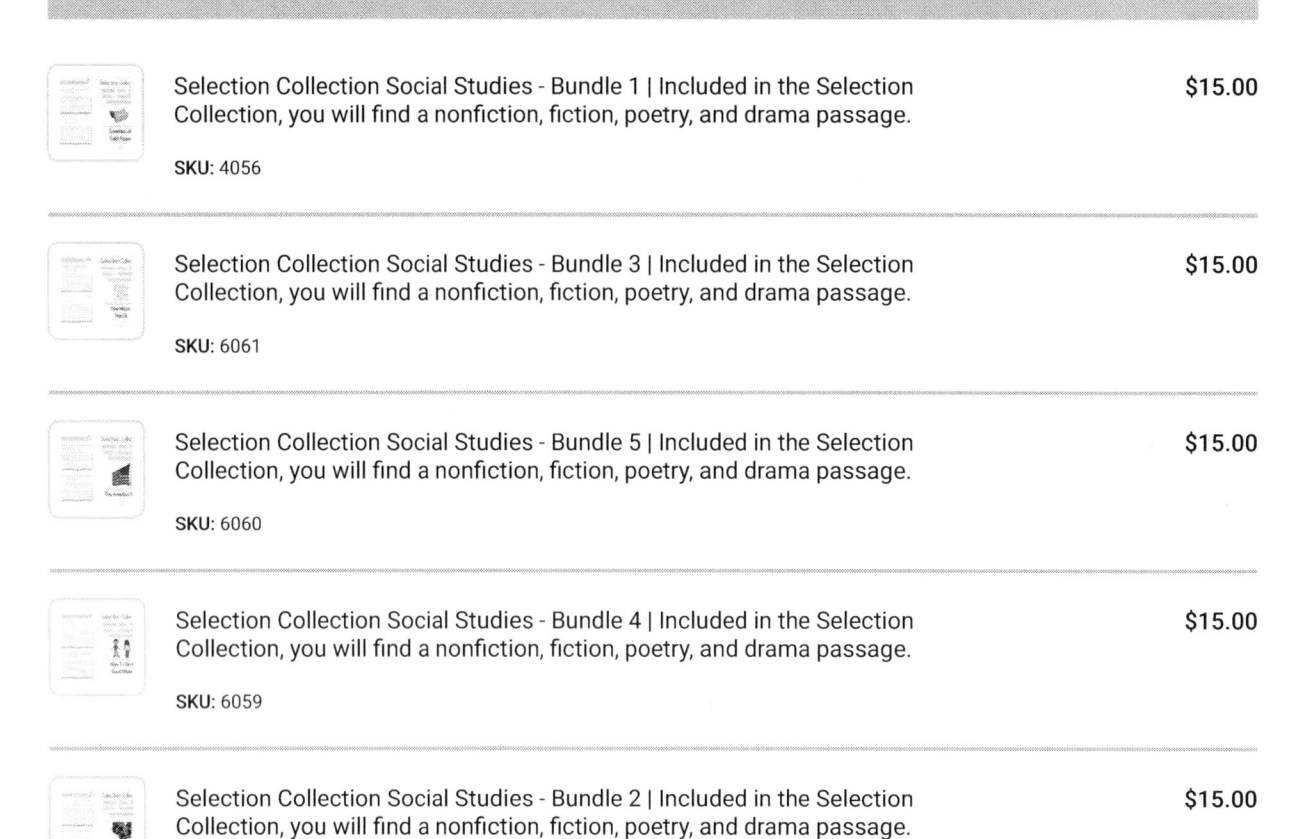

SELECTION COLLECTION - SOCIAL STUDIES - BUNDLES

Selection Collection Social Studies - Bundle 1 | Included in the Selection Collection, you will find a nonfiction, fiction, poetry, and drama passage. **SKU:** 4056		$15.00
Selection Collection Social Studies - Bundle 3 | Included in the Selection Collection, you will find a nonfiction, fiction, poetry, and drama passage. **SKU:** 6061		$15.00
Selection Collection Social Studies - Bundle 5 | Included in the Selection Collection, you will find a nonfiction, fiction, poetry, and drama passage. **SKU:** 6060		$15.00
Selection Collection Social Studies - Bundle 4 | Included in the Selection Collection, you will find a nonfiction, fiction, poetry, and drama passage. **SKU:** 6059		$15.00
Selection Collection Social Studies - Bundle 2 | Included in the Selection Collection, you will find a nonfiction, fiction, poetry, and drama passage. **SKU:** 4057		$15.00

SELECTION COLLECTION - SOCIAL STUDIES - BUNDLES

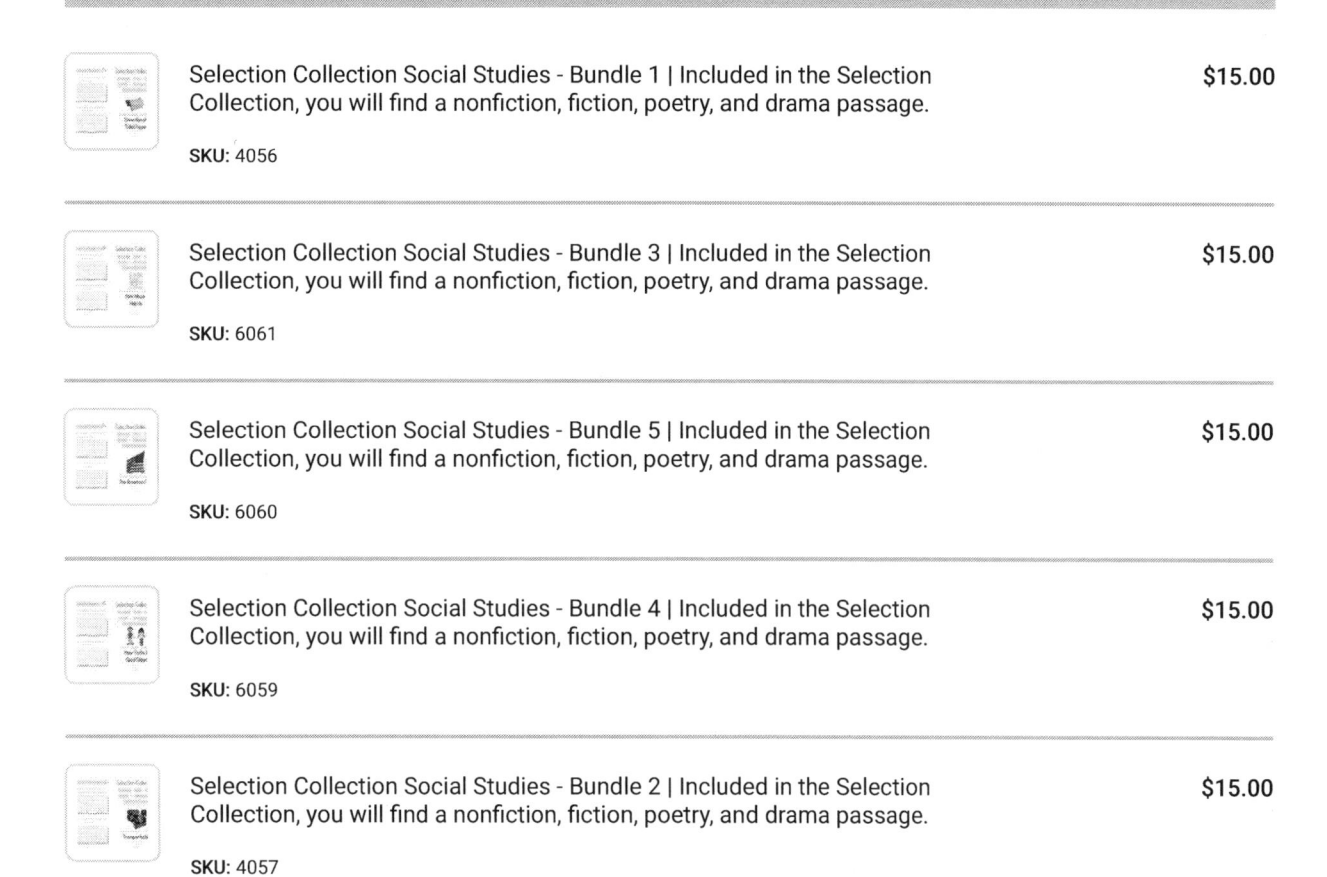

Selection Collection Social Studies - Bundle 1 | Included in the Selection Collection, you will find a nonfiction, fiction, poetry, and drama passage. $15.00

SKU: 4056

Selection Collection Social Studies - Bundle 3 | Included in the Selection Collection, you will find a nonfiction, fiction, poetry, and drama passage. $15.00

SKU: 6061

Selection Collection Social Studies - Bundle 5 | Included in the Selection Collection, you will find a nonfiction, fiction, poetry, and drama passage. $15.00

SKU: 6060

Selection Collection Social Studies - Bundle 4 | Included in the Selection Collection, you will find a nonfiction, fiction, poetry, and drama passage. $15.00

SKU: 6059

Selection Collection Social Studies - Bundle 2 | Included in the Selection Collection, you will find a nonfiction, fiction, poetry, and drama passage. $15.00

SKU: 4057

SLIDE SHOWS

Prompt to Product - Interactive ECR SKU: 6067		$20.00
Mini Classroom Lesson	TRACKS SKU: 4068		$5.00
Sentence Weather - Interactive Weekly Forecast SKU: 6066		$10.00
Mini Classroom Lesson	The Writing Process SKU: 4064		$5.00
Mini Classroom Lesson	Vowels SKU: 4054		$5.00

SPANISH RESOURCES

	Alliteration Ambrosia - Spanish	This resource is great for grades 4-6. **SKU:** 2040	$5.00
	Character Traits - Spanish	This resource is great for grades 2-3. **SKU:** 2029	$5.00
	Home to School - TEKS 10A	SPANISH	This TEKS-specific letter can be used based on data you have gathered from practice assessments and other classroom activities. **SKU:** 3007	$1.00
	I - Write Foldable	SPANISH	This item contains a three-part foldable to create a movable I-Write Plan. The foldable is adjustable based on how much textual evidence a student would like to use. **SKU:** 3078	$5.00
	Parts of Speech - Spanish	This resource is great for grades 2-3. **SKU:** 2039	$7.00
	Passage Practice : Drama - 3rd Grade - Home for the Holidays	SPANISH **SKU:** 5099	$5.00
	Passage Practice : Drama - 3rd Grade - Summer Troubles	SPANISH **SKU:** 3015	$5.00
	Passage Practice: Drama - 4th Grade - Garner State Park	SPANISH **SKU:** 8013	$5.00

Passage Practice: Drama - 4th Grade - Home for the Holidays | Spanish SKU: 6008		$5.00
Passage Practice: Drama - 5th Grade - Garner State Park | SPANISH SKU: 8023		$5.00
Passage Practice: Drama - 5th Grade - Home for the Holidays | Spanish SKU: 6018		$5.00
Passage Practice: Fiction - 3rd Grade - A Winter's Gift | SPANISH SKU: 6001		$5.00
Passage Practice: Fiction - 4th Grade - A Winter's Gift | Spanish SKU: 6010		$5.00
Passage Practice: Fiction - 5th Grade - A Winter's Gift | Spanish SKU: 6020		$5.00
Passage Practice: Nonfiction - 3rd Grade - Benefits of Peppermint | SPANISH SKU: 6003		$5.00
Passage Practice: Nonfiction - 3rd Grade - History of the Panama Canal | SPANISH SKU: 8007		$5.00
Passage Practice: Nonfiction - 3rd Grade - Hoover Dam | SPANISH SKU: 8009		$5.00
Passage Practice: Nonfiction - 3rd Grade - How the Magic is Born | Spanish SKU: 6005		$5.00
Passage Practice: Nonfiction - 4th Grade - Cajun Navy | SPANISH SKU: 8015		$5.00

	Passage Practice: Nonfiction - 4th Grade - History of the Panama Canal | SPANISH SKU: 8017	$5.00
	Passage Practice: Nonfiction - 4th Grade - Hoover Dam | SPANISH SKU: 8019	$5.00
	Passage Practice: Nonfiction - 4th Grade - How the Magic is Born | Spanish SKU: 6014	$5.00
	Passage Practice: Nonfiction - 5th Grade - Benefits of Peppermint | Spanish SKU: 6022	$5.00
	Passage Practice: Nonfiction - 5th Grade - History of the Panama Canal | SPANISH SKU: 8025	$5.00
	Passage Practice: Nonfiction - 5th Grade - Hoover Dam | SPANISH SKU: 8027	$5.00
	Passage Practice: Nonfiction - 5th Grade - How the Magic is Born | Spanish SKU: 6024	$5.00
	Passage Practice: Nonfiction - 5th Grade - The Cajun Navy | SPANISH SKU: 8029	$5.00
	Passage Practice: Set 4 - 4th Grade | Spanish SKU: 6016	$15.00
	Passage Practice: Set 4 - 5th Grade | Spanish SKU: 6026	$15.00
	Passage Practice: Set 7 - 4th Grade | SPANISH SKU: 8021	$15.00

Practice Passage : Drama – 3rd Grade – Garner State Park | SPANISH SKU: 8003		$5.00
Practice Passage : Drama – 3rd Grade –The Quarter-SPANISH SKU: 4087		$5.00
Practice Passage : Drama – 4th Grade –The Quarter-SPANISH SKU: 4094		$5.00
Practice Passage : Drama – 5th Grade – Summer Troubles | SPANISH SKU: 3080		$5.00
Practice Passage : Drama – 5th Grade – The Quarter-SPANISH SKU: 5013		$5.00
Practice Passage : Fiction - 3rd Grade - The Award | SPANISH SKU: 3017		$5.00
Practice Passage : Fiction - 3rd Grade - William Shakespeare | SPANISH SKU: 3027		$5.00
Practice Passage : Fiction - 5th Grade - The Award | SPANISH SKU: 4018		$5.00
Practice Passage : Fiction - 5th Grade - William Shakespeare | SPANISH SKU: 4022		$5.00
Practice Passage : Fiction – 3rd Grade – The New Addition-SPANISH SKU: 4089		$5.00
Practice Passage : Fiction – 4th Grade – The New Addition-SPANISH SKU: 4099		$5.00

Practice Passage : Fiction – 5th Grade – Andria-SPANISH SKU: 5015		$5.00
Practice Passage : Fiction – 5th Grade – The New Addition-SPANISH SKU: 5017		$5.00
Practice Passage : Non Fiction – 4th Grade – The History of Thanksgiving-SPANISH SKU: 5006		$5.00
Practice Passage : Nonfiction - 3rd Grade - Sam Walton-From the Great Depression to Billionaire | SPANISH SKU: 3022		$5.00
Practice Passage : Nonfiction - 5th Grade - Sam Walton - From the Great Depression to Billionaire | SPANISH SKU: 4020		$5.00
Practice Passage : Nonfiction – 3rd Grade – Patrick Mahomes | SPANISH SKU: 4075		$5.00
Practice Passage : Nonfiction – 3rd Grade – The Cajun Navy | SPANISH SKU: 8005		$5.00
Practice Passage : Nonfiction – 3rd Grade – The Invention of the Crayola | SPANISH SKU: 4073		$5.00
Practice Passage : Nonfiction – 3rd Grade – Why Leaves Change Colors | SPANISH SKU: 4079		$5.00
Practice Passage : Poetry – 3rd Grade – Autumn's Poem | SPANISH SKU: 4077		$5.00
Practice Passage : Set 1 - 3rd Grade | SPANISH SKU: 4069		$15.00

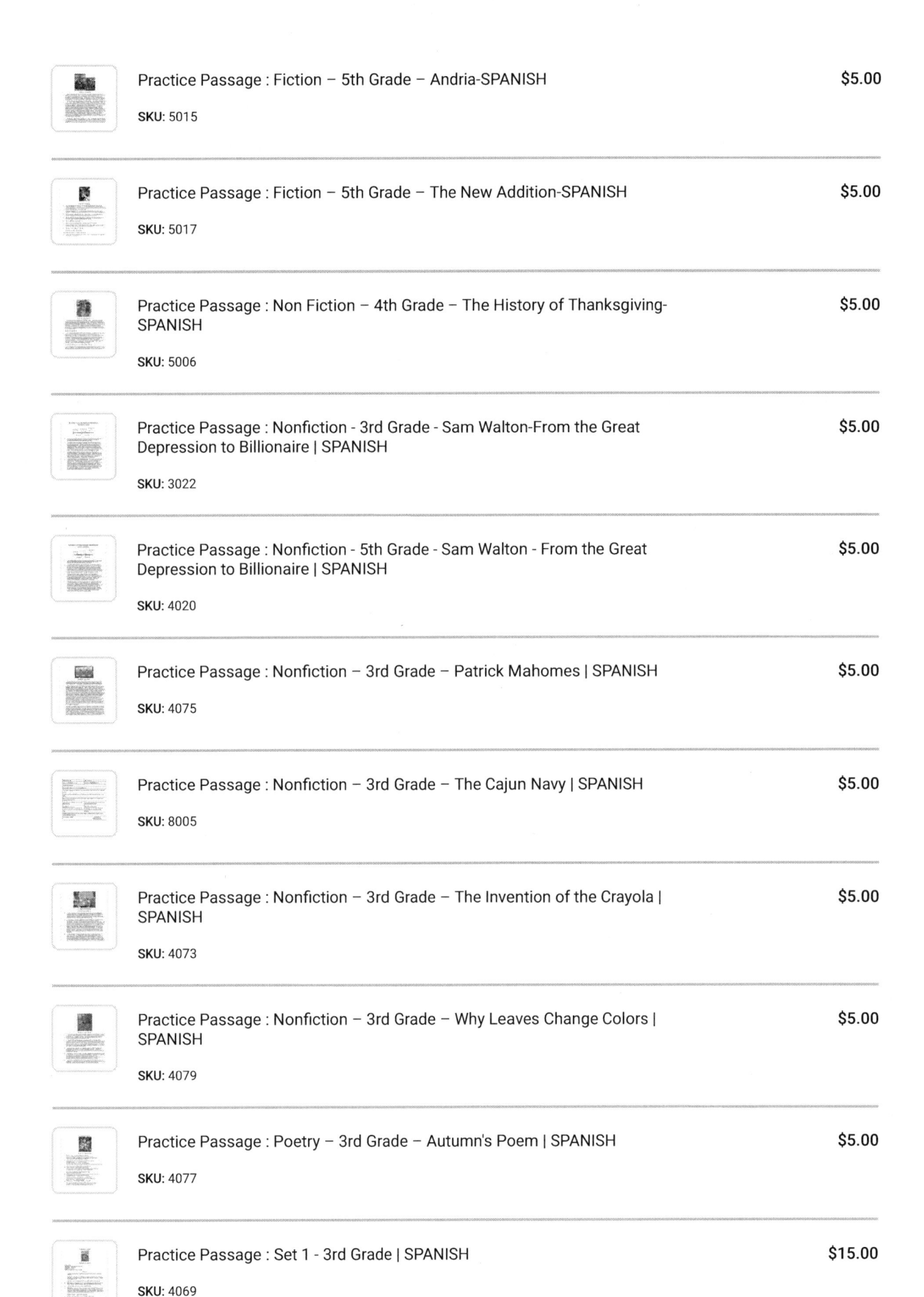

	Practice Passage : Set 1 - 3rd Grade-SPANISH SKU: 4090	$15.00
	Practice Passage : Set 1 - 4th Grade | SPANISH SKU: 4070	$15.00
	Practice Passage : Set 1 - 5th Grade | SPANISH SKU: 4071	$15.00
	Practice Passage : Set 2 - 3rd Grade SKU: 4080	$15.00
	Practice Passage : Set 2 - 3rd Grade | SPANISH SKU: 4081	$15.00
	Practice Passage : Set 3 - 4th Grade-SPANISH SKU: 5008	$15.00
	Practice Passage : Set 3- 5th Grade-SPANISH SKU: 6051	$15.00
	Practice Passage : Set 7 - 3rd Grade | SPANISH SKU: 8011	$15.00
	Practice Passage: Drama-4th Grade- Summer Troubles | SPANISH SKU: 3047	$5.00
	Practice Passage: Fiction – 4th Grade- The Award | SPANISH SKU: 3049	$5.00
	Practice Passage: Fiction- 4th Grade- William Shakespeare | SPANISH SKU: 3054	$5.00

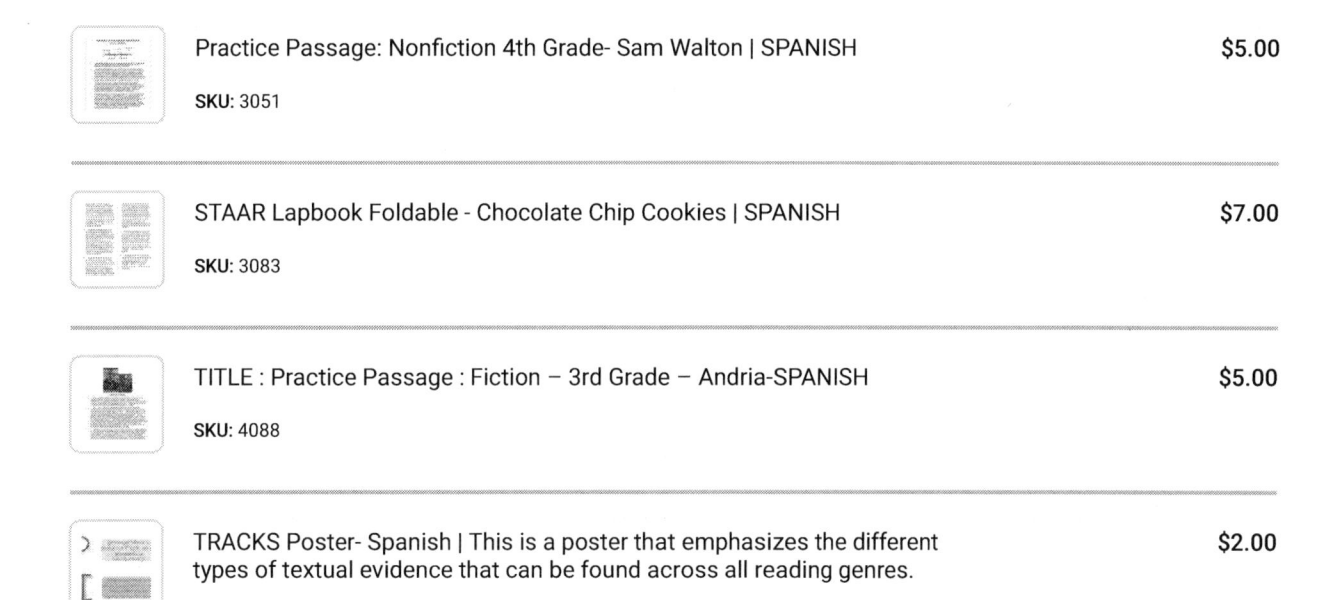

	Practice Passage: Nonfiction 4th Grade- Sam Walton | SPANISH SKU: 3051	$5.00
	STAAR Lapbook Foldable - Chocolate Chip Cookies | SPANISH SKU: 3083	$7.00
	TITLE : Practice Passage : Fiction – 3rd Grade – Andria-SPANISH SKU: 4088	$5.00
	TRACKS Poster- Spanish | This is a poster that emphasizes the different types of textual evidence that can be found across all reading genres. SKU: 3068	$2.00

STAAR RESOURCES

	2023 Released STAAR Test Data: Editing & Revising (Grades 3–8) SKU: 1126	$5.00
	2024 Released STAAR Test Data: Editing & Revising (Grades 3–8) SKU: 1127	$5.00
	Academic STAAR Vocabulary (2022-2024) SKU: 1114	$8.00
	Basic ECR Response for Struggling Writers SKU: 1105	$0.00
	CSI Rate the Evidence SKU: 1123	$0.00
	ECR Companion Pack SKU: 1124	$0.00
	Finding Evidence - Where Did You Get Those Kicks? SKU: 1104	$0.00
	General Companion Pack SKU: 1125	$0.00
	STAAR Question Stems (2022–2024) — 10th Grade SKU: 1122	$3.00

	STAAR Question Stems (2022–2024) — 3rd Grade SKU: 1115	$3.00
	STAAR Question Stems (2022–2024) — 4th Grade SKU: 1116	$3.00
	STAAR Question Stems (2022–2024) — 5th Grade SKU: 1117	$3.00
	STAAR Question Stems (2022–2024) — 6th Grade SKU: 1118	$3.00
	STAAR Question Stems (2022–2024) — 7th Grade SKU: 1119	$3.00
	STAAR Question Stems (2022–2024) — 8th Grade SKU: 1120	$3.00
	STAAR Question Stems (2022–2024) — 9th Grade SKU: 1121	$3.00
	TEKS to CCSS ELAR Crosswalk Document - 1st Grade SKU: 1132	$5.00
	TEKS to CCSS ELAR Crosswalk Document - 2nd Grade SKU: 1106	$5.00
	TEKS to CCSS ELAR Crosswalk Document - 3rd Grade SKU: 1107	$5.00
	TEKS to CCSS ELAR Crosswalk Document - 4th Grade SKU: 1108	$5.00

TEKS to CCSS ELAR Crosswalk Document - 5th Grade SKU: 1109		$5.00
TEKS to CCSS ELAR Crosswalk Document - 6th Grade SKU: 1110		$5.00
TEKS to CCSS ELAR Crosswalk Document - 7th Grade SKU: 1111		$5.00
TEKS to CCSS ELAR Crosswalk Document - 8th Grade SKU: 1112		$5.00
TEKS to CCSS ELAR Crosswalk Document - 9th-10th SKU: 1130		$5.00
TEKS to CCSS ELAR Crosswalk Document - Kindergarten SKU: 1131		$5.00
TEKS to CCSS ELAR Crosswalk Document - TEKS Not Used in CCSS SKU: 1113		$5.00

TEKS LESSON PLANS - 1ST GRADE

	1st Grade	Unit 8A: Informational Text SKU: 5086	$20.00
	1st Grade	Unit 2: Text Connections SKU: 5025	$20.00
	1st Grade	Unit 1: Literary Foundations SKU: 4051	$20.00
	1st Grade	Unit 11: Bringing It All Together SKU: 5090	$20.00
	1st Grade	Unit 10: Persuasive Text SKU: 5089	$20.00
	1st Grade	Unit 9: Poetry SKU: 5088	$20.00
	1st Grade	Unit 8B: Diving Further Into Informational SKU: 5087	$20.00
	1st Grade	Unit 7B: Literary Text SKU: 5085	$20.00
	1st Grade	Unit 7A: Drama SKU: 5084	$20.00

1st Grade | Unit 6: Higher Level Reading — $20.00
SKU: 5083

1st Grade | Unit 4: Reading Comprehension — $20.00
SKU: 5027

1st Grade | Unit 3: Generating Questions — $20.00
SKU: 5026

TEKS LESSON PLANS - 2ND GRADE

	2nd Grade	Unit 6A: Drama **SKU:** 5091	$20.00
	2nd Grade	Unit 4: Reading Comprehension **SKU:** 5030	$20.00
	2nd Grade	Unit 3: Generating Questions **SKU:** 5029	$20.00
	2nd Grade	Unit 1: Literary Foundations **SKU:** 4058	$20.00
	2nd Grade	Unit 10: Bringing It All Together **SKU:** 5097	$20.00
	2nd Grade	Unit 9: Persuasive Text **SKU:** 5096	$20.00
	2nd Grade	Unit 8: Poetry **SKU:** 5095	$20.00
	2nd Grade	Unit 7B: Inquiry and Research **SKU:** 5094	$20.00
	2nd Grade	Unit 7A: Informational Text **SKU:** 5093	$20.00

	2nd Grade	Unit 6B: Literary Text SKU: 5092	$20.00
	2nd Grade	Unit 2: Text Connections SKU: 5028	$20.00

TEKS LESSON PLANS - 3RD GRADE

3rd Grade | Unit 1: Literary Foundations — $20.00
SKU: 4060

3rd Grade | Unit 2A: Author's Purpose and Craft — $20.00
SKU: 5031

3rd Grade | Unit 3B: Literary Text — $20.00
SKU: 5036

3rd Grade | Unit 2C: The Power of Words — $20.00
SKU: 5034

3rd Grade | Unit 3A: Voice — $20.00
SKU: 5035

3rd Grade | Unit 2B: Journey of Thought — $20.00
SKU: 5032

3rd Grade | Unit 7: Argumentative Text — $20.00
SKU: 5040

3rd Grade | Unit 6: Poetry — $20.00
SKU: 5039

3rd Grade | Unit 5: Drama — $20.00
SKU: 5038

3rd Grade | Unit 4: Informational Text $20.00

SKU: 5037

3rd Grade | Unit 9: Research and Inquiry $20.00

SKU: 5042

3rd Grade | Unit 8: Response Across Genres $20.00

SKU: 5041

TEKS LESSON PLANS - 4TH GRADE

	4th Grade | Unit 1: Literary Foundations SKU: 4061	$20.00
	4th Grade | Unit 8: Response Across Genres SKU: 5052	$20.00
	4th Grade | Unit 3A: Literary Elements SKU: 5046	$20.00
	4th Grade | Unit 2C: The Power of Words SKU: 5045	$20.00
	4th Grade | Unit 2A: Author's Purpose and Craft SKU: 5043	$20.00
	4th Grade | Unit 9: Research and Inquiry SKU: 5053	$20.00
	4th Grade | Unit 7: Argumentative Text SKU: 5051	$20.00
	4th Grade | Unit 6: Poetry SKU: 5050	$20.00
	4th Grade | Unit 5: Drama SKU: 5049	$20.00

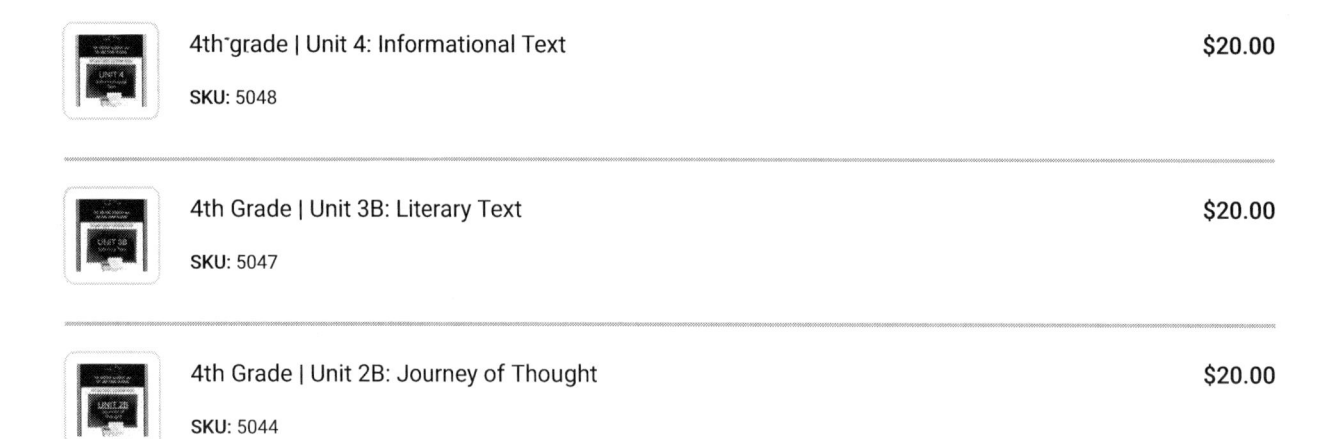

4th grade | Unit 4: Informational Text **SKU:** 5048		$20.00
4th Grade | Unit 3B: Literary Text **SKU:** 5047		$20.00
4th Grade | Unit 2B: Journey of Thought **SKU:** 5044		$20.00

TEKS LESSON PLANS - 5TH GRADE

5th Grade	Unit 1: Literary Foundations SKU: 4062		$20.00

5th Grade | Unit 1: Literary Foundations
SKU: 4062 — $20.00

5th Grade | Unit 5: Drama
SKU: 5060 — $20.00

5th Grade | Unit 7: Argumentative Text
SKU: 5062 — $20.00

5th Grade | Unit 8: Response Across Genres
SKU: 5063 — $20.00

5th Grade | Unit 6: Poetry
SKU: 5061 — $20.00

5th Grade | Unit 4: Informational Text
SKU: 5059 — $20.00

5th Grade | Unit 3B: Literary Text
SKU: 5058 — $20.00

5th Grade | Unit 3A: Literary Text
SKU: 5057 — $20.00

5th Grade | Unit 2C: The Power of Words
SKU: 5056 — $20.00

5th Grade | Unit 2B: Journey of Thought $20.00
SKU: 5055

5th Grade | Unit 2A: Author's Purpose and Craft $20.00
SKU: 5054

TEKS LESSON PLANS - 6TH - 8TH GRADE

	6th-8th Grade	Unit 4: Argumentative Text SKU: 5067	$20.00
	6th-8th Grade	Unit 2B: Poetry and Drama SKU: 5065	$20.00
	6th-8th Grade	Unit 6: Research SKU: 5069	$20.00
	6th-8th Grade	Unit 5: Response Across Genres SKU: 5068	$20.00
	6th-8th Grade	Unit 3: Informational Text SKU: 5066	$20.00
	6th-8th Grade	Unit 2A: Literary Text SKU: 5064	$20.00
	6th-8th Grade	Unit 1: Literary Foundations SKU: 4063	$20.00

TEKS REWARD CERTIFICATES

Way To Tackle The TEKS! Certificate - TEKS 9A - 9F | This TEKS certificate isn't just a paper; it represents students' effort, determination, and hard work.　　　　　$3.00

SKU: 7098

Way To Tackle The TEKS! Certificate - TEKS 8A - 8D | This TEKS certificate isn't just a paper; it represents students' effort, determination, and hard work.　　　　　$3.00

SKU: 7097

Way To Tackle The TEKS! Certificate - TEKS 10A - 10G | This TEKS certificate isn't just a paper; it represents students' effort, determination, and hard work.　　　　　$3.00

SKU: 7099

Way To Tackle The TEKS! Certificate - TEKS 7A - 7F | This TEKS certificate isn't just a paper; it represents students' effort, determination, and hard work.　　　　　$3.00

SKU: 7096

Way To Tackle The TEKS! Certificate - TEKS 6A - 6I | This TEKS certificate isn't just a paper; it represents students' effort, determination, and hard work.　　　　　$3.00

SKU: 7095

TEKS TASK CARDS

TEKS Task Cards : 10A - Poetry SKU: 3038		$3.00
TEKS Task Cards: 10A - Drama SKU: 4026		$3.00
TEKS Task Cards: 10A - Nonfiction SKU: 4025		$3.00
TEKS Task Cards : 7C – Science – Set 1 SKU: 4027		$15.00
TEKS Task Cards : 10A – Social Studies – Set 1 SKU: 4029		$15.00
TEKS Task Cards: 10A - Fiction SKU: 4024		$3.00
TEKS Task Cards: 9Di - Social Studies - Set 3 SKU: 8037		$5.00
TEKS Task Cards: 9Di - Science - Set 3 SKU: 8036		$5.00
TEKS Task Cards : 7D – Social Studies – Set 1 SKU: 5002		$15.00

TEKS Task Cards : 7C – Social Studies – Set 1 **SKU:** 5009		$15.00
TEKS Task Cards : 6F – Social Studies – Set 1 **SKU:** 5010		$15.00
TEKS Task Cards : 6E Dual Passage – Social Studies – Set 4 **SKU:** 5003		$15.00
TEKS Task Cards : 10A – Science – Set 1 **SKU:** 5011		$15.00

TRAININGS

	Training - Teach Big Classroom Lessons SKU: 1242	$1,990.00
	Student Training Camp - ECR Written Constructed Response CAMP SKU: 1182	$1,900.00
	Student Training Camp - Reading Comprehension CAMP SKU: 1181	$1,900.00
	Student Training Camp - Revising CAMP SKU: 1180	$1,900.00
	Student Training Camp - Editing CAMP SKU: 1179	$1,900.00
	Student Training Camp - TEKS Vocabulary Training SKU: 1178	$1,900.00
	Training - Ride the WAVE (Virtual) SKU: 1176	$500.00
	Training - Getting in SHAPE: Securing How All People Excel (Virtual) SKU: 1175	$1,850.00
	Training - Teach BIG for SLIFE Students (Virtual) SKU: 1174	$1,850.00

Training - Dual Language Duo (Virtual) SKU: 1173		$1,850.00
Training - Short and Extended Constructed Response (Virtual) SKU: 1172		$1,850.00
Training - ELAR TEKS Training (Virtual) SKU: 1171		$1,850.00
Training - The 4 Dimensions of Reading (Virtual) SKU: 1170		$1,850.00
Training - Top 10 ELAR Bundle (Virtual) SKU: 1169		$1,850.00
Training - Editing and Revising (Virtual) SKU: 1168		$1,850.00
Training - Vocabulary and Fluency (Virtual) SKU: 1167		$1,850.00
Training - Phonics Bundle (Virtual) SKU: 1166		$1,850.00
Training - Teach BIG for SLIFE Students (In Kemah) SKU: 1165		$100.00
Training - Dual Language Duo (In Kemah) SKU: 1164		$100.00
Training - Short and Extended Constructed Response (In Kemah) SKU: 1163		$100.00

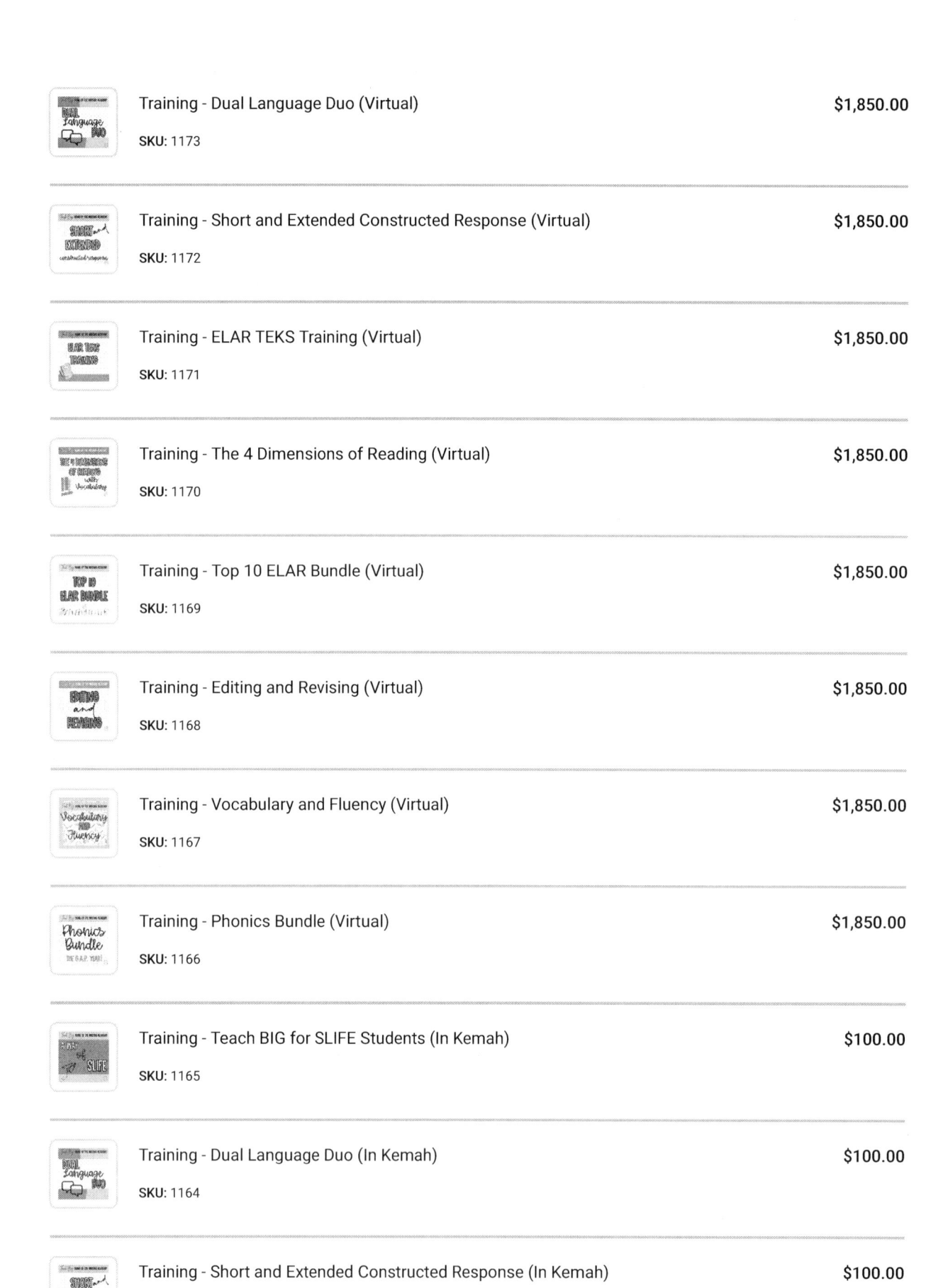

	Training - ELAR TEKS Training (In Kemah) SKU: 1162	$100.00
	Training - The 4 Dimensions of Reading (In Kemah) SKU: 1161	$100.00
	Training - Top 10 ELAR Bundle (In Kemah) SKU: 1160	$300.00
	Training - Editing and Revising (In Kemah) SKU: 1159	$100.00
	Training - Vocabulary and Fluency (In Kemah) SKU: 1158	$100.00
	Training - Phonics Bundle (In Kemah) SKU: 1157	$200.00
	Training - Get in SHAPE: Securing How All People Excel (At the Ranch) SKU: 1156	$100.00
	Training - Teach BIG for SLIFE Students (At the Ranch) SKU: 1155	$400.00
	Training - Dual Language Duo (At the Ranch) SKU: 1154	$400.00
	Training - Short & Constructed Response (At the Ranch) SKU: 1153	$400.00
	Training - ELAR TEKS Training (At the Ranch) SKU: 1152	$400.00

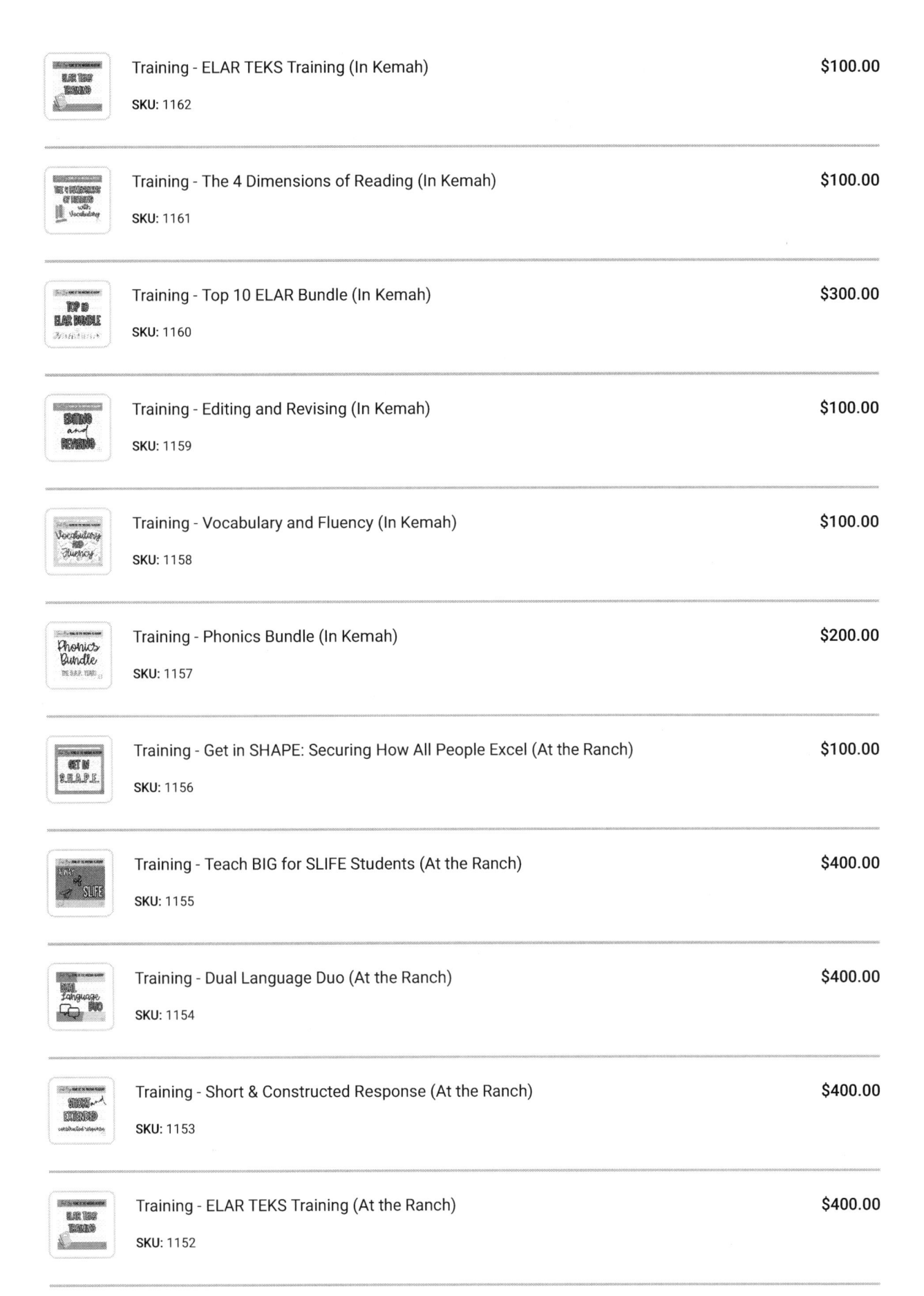

Training - The 4 Dimensions of Reading (At the Ranch) SKU: 1151		$400.00
Training - Top 10 ELAR Bundle (At the Ranch) SKU: 1150		$500.00
Training - Editing and Revising (At the Ranch) SKU: 1149		$400.00
Training - Vocabulary and Fluency (At the Ranch) SKU: 1148		$400.00
Training - Phonics Bundle (At the Ranch) SKU: 1147		$400.00
Training - Getting in SHAPE: Securing How All People Excel (at your campus) SKU: 1146		$1,990.00
Training - Teach BIG for SLIFE Students (at your campus) SKU: 1145		$1,990.00
Training - Dual Language Duo (at your campus) SKU: 1144		$1,990.00
Training - Short & Extended Constructed Response (at your campus) SKU: 1143		$1,990.00
Training - ELAR TEKS Training (at your campus) SKU: 1142		$1,990.00
Training - The 4 Dimensions of Reading (at your campus) SKU: 1141		$1,990.00

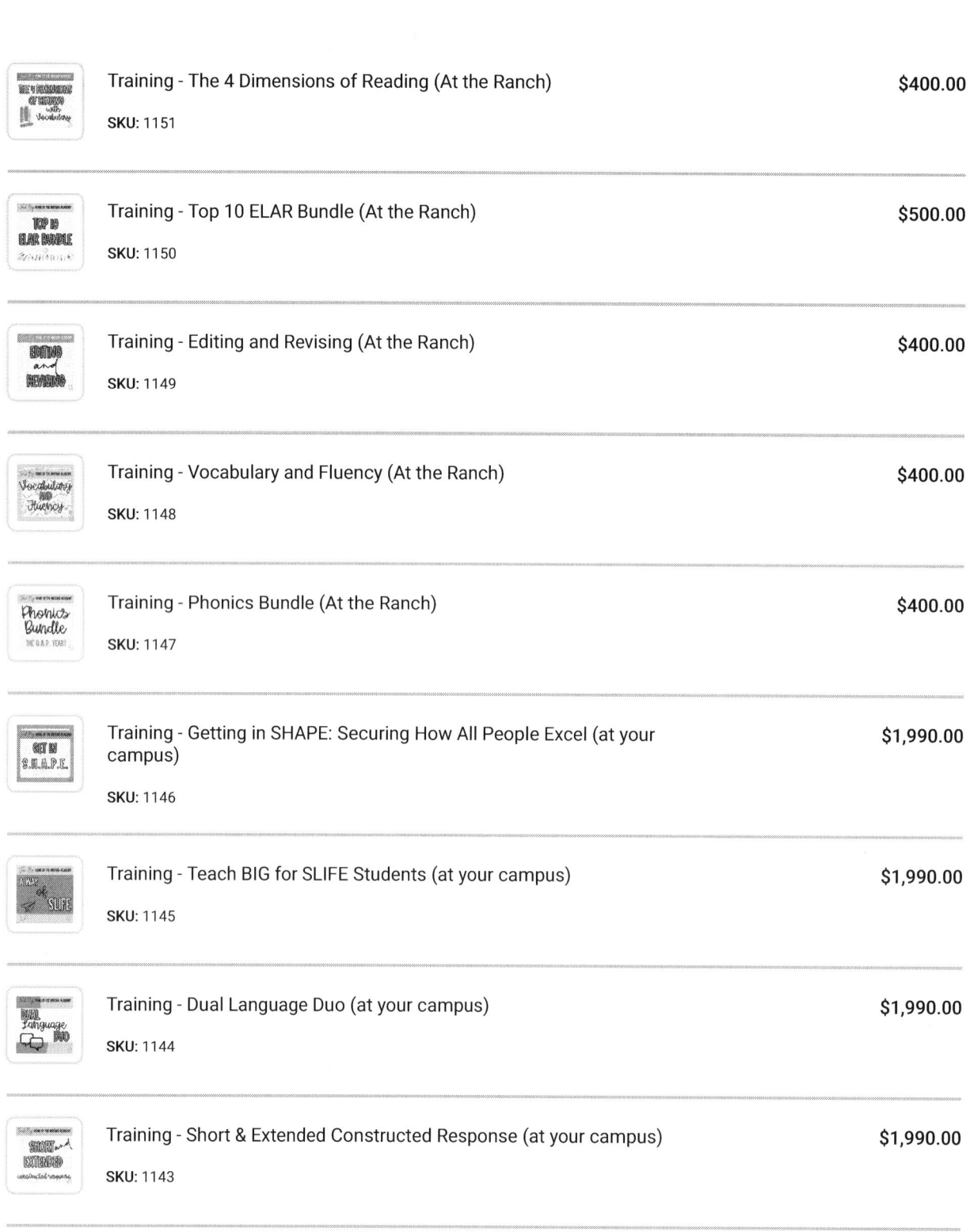

Training - Top 10 ELAR Bundle (at your campus) SKU: 1140		$1,990.00
Training - Editing and Revising (at your campus) SKU: 1139		$1,990.00
Training - Vocabulary and Fluency (at your campus) SKU: 1138		$1,990.00
Training - Phonics Bundle (at your campus) SKU: 1137		$1,990.00
Inservice Chart with Pricing SKU: 1134		$0.00

TUTORIAL ACTIVITIES

	1st Person vs 3rd Person Activity	This resource is great for grades 4-6. SKU: 2034	$2.00
	Adjective Postcards	This resource is great for grades 4-6. SKU: 2007	$5.00
	Adjective Word Search	This resource is great for grades 2-3. SKU: 2003	$2.00
	Advertising with Purpose - Ethos, Logos, Pathos	This resource is great for grades 7-8. SKU: 2031	$5.00
	Alliteration Ambrosia Activity	This resource is great for grades 4-6. SKU: 2015	$5.00
	Antonym Acting!	This resource is great for grades 2-3. SKU: 2014	$5.00
	Author's Purpose Game Board	This resource is great for grades 4-6. SKU: 1099	$5.00
	Capitalization Trashketball Activity	This resource is great for grades 2-3. SKU: 1098	$5.00
	Capitalizing Proper Nouns	This resource is great for grades 4-6. SKU: 2006	$1.00

	Character Traits	This resource is great for grades 2-3. SKU: 2028	$5.00
	Contraction Puzzles Activity	This resource is great for grades 2-3. SKU: 2002	$2.00
	Correlative Conjunctions	This resource is great for grades 4-6. SKU: 2018	$5.00
	Counter Arguments	This resource is great for grades 7-8. SKU: 2033	$2.00
	Fairy-Tale Characteristics	This resource is great for grades 2-3. SKU: 2030	$5.00
	Genres Bingo	This resource is great for grades 7-8. SKU: 2025	$5.00
	Homophone Crossword	This resource is great for grades 4-6. SKU: 1097	$2.00
	Literary Devices Bingo	This resource is great for grades 7-8. SKU: 1095	$7.00
	Marking the Punctuation	This resource is great for grades 4-6. SKU: 2035	$2.00
	Memorize It!	This resource is great for grades 7-8. SKU: 2022	$2.00
	Missing Punctuation Activity	This resource is great for grades 4-6. SKU: 1096	$2.00

Parts of Speech Activity | This resource is great for grades 2-3. SKU: 2012		$7.00
Phonemes Haircuts Activity | This resource is great for grades 2-3. SKU: 2004		$2.00
Plural Pies | This resource is great for grades 4-6. SKU: 2024		$1.00
Prefix Bingo | This resource is great for grades 2-3. SKU: 2041		$7.00
Prepositions "4 in a Row" Activity | This resource is great for grades 7-8. SKU: 2010		$2.00
Punting Punctuation Activity | This resource is great for grades 7-8. SKU: 2011		$7.00
Racing Through The Dictionary! | This resource is great for grades 7-8. SKU: 2001		$1.00
Rhyme Schemes | This resource is great for grades 2-3. SKU: 2027		$1.00
Rhyme Time | A fun activity that can be used in a station or small group. SKU: 1049		$5.00
Roll a Prefix Activity | This resource is great for grades 4-6. SKU: 2008		$2.00
Rolling Personifications Activity | This resource is great for grades 7-8. SKU: 2000		$1.00

Rounding Up The Nouns | This resource is great for grades 4-6. **SKU:** 2016		$2.00
Silent Letters | This resource is great for grades 2-3. **SKU:** 2013		$1.00
Singular & Plural Nouns Cookies Activity | This resource is great for grades 2-3. **SKU:** 2005		$5.00
Sort the Sources! | This resource is great for grades 4-6. **SKU:** 2023		$2.00
Spin for the Audience! | This resource is great for grades 7-8. **SKU:** 2021		$5.00
Storytelling Adverbs | This resource is great for grades 7-8. **SKU:** 2032		$2.00
Suffixes | This resource is great for grades 4-6. **SKU:** 2038		$5.00
Thesis Tic Tac Toe | This resource is great for grades 4-6. **SKU:** 2026		$5.00
Verb Tents Activity | This resource is great for grades 7-8. **SKU:** 2009		$5.00
Whale Citing | This resource is great for grades 7-8. **SKU:** 2020		$2.00
"Looking into the Future" Foreshadowing Activity | This resource is great for grades 7-8. **SKU:** 2017		$2.00

VOCABULARY

	Character Traits	This resource is great for grades 2-3. SKU: 2028	$5.00
	Genres Bingo	This resource is great for grades 7-8. SKU: 2025	$5.00
	Look It Up! SKU: 9041	$12.00
	Out of Sorts SKU: 9040	$12.00
	Prefix Bingo	This resource is great for grades 2-3. SKU: 2041	$7.00
	Racing Through The Dictionary!	This resource is great for grades 7-8. SKU: 2001	$1.00
	Rhyme Time	A fun activity that can be used in a station or small group. SKU: 1049	$5.00
	Roll a Prefix Activity	This resource is great for grades 4-6. SKU: 2008	$2.00
	Silent Letters	This resource is great for grades 2-3. SKU: 2013	$1.00

	Six Syllables Drama SKU: 8035	$10.00
	Sort the Sources! | This resource is great for grades 4-6. SKU: 2023	$2.00
	Spin for the Audience! | This resource is great for grades 7-8. SKU: 2021	$5.00
	Suffixes | This resource is great for grades 4-6. SKU: 2038	$5.00
	Vocabulary through the DECADES SKU: 5033	$0.00
	Whale Citing | This resource is great for grades 7-8. SKU: 2020	$2.00

WORD FAMILY BOOKLETS

Word Family Book - ag | This word family booklet emphasizes the word family - ag. It goes great in a station or as individual work sent home to further the home to school connection. $1.00

SKU: 1011

Word Family Book - am | This word family booklet emphasizes the word family - am. It goes great in a station or as individual work sent home to further the home to school connection. $1.00

SKU: 1005

Word Family Book - ame | This word family booklet emphasizes the word family - ame. It goes great in a station or as individual work sent home to further the home to school connection. $1.00

SKU: 1004

Word Family Book - ap | This word family booklet emphasizes the word family - ap. It goes great in a station or as individual work sent home to further the home to school connection. $1.00

SKU: 1016

Word Family Book - ool | This word family booklet emphasizes the word family - ool. It goes great in a station or as individual work sent home to further the home to school connection. $1.00

SKU: 1060

Word Family Book-oke | This word family booklet emphasizes the word family — oke. It goes great in a station or as individual work sent home to further the home to school connection. $1.00

SKU: 1055

Word Family Books - eep. | This word family booklet emphasizes the word family — eep. It goes great in a station or as individual work sent home to further the home to school connection. $1.00

SKU: 1024

Word Family Books - ack | This word family booklet emphasizes the word family — ack. It goes great in a station or as individual work sent home to further the home to school connection.

SKU: 1013

$1.00

Word Family Books - ad | This word family booklet emphasizes the word family — ad. It goes great in a station or as individual work sent home to further the home to school connection.

SKU: 1012

$1.00

Word Family Books - age | This word family booklet emphasizes the word family — age. It goes great in a station or as individual work sent home to further the home to school connection.

SKU: 1010

$1.00

Word Family Books - ail | This word family booklet emphasizes the word family — ail. It goes great in a station or as individual work sent home to further the home to school connection.

SKU: 1009

$1.00

Word Family Books - ake | This word family booklet emphasizes the word family — ake. It goes great in a station or as individual work sent home to further the home to school connection.

SKU: 1007

$1.00

Word Family Books - an | This word family booklet emphasizes the word family — an. It goes great in a station or as individual work sent home to further the home to school connection.

SKU: 1014

$1.00

Word Family Books - ane | This word family booklet emphasizes the word family — ane. It goes great in a station or as individual work sent home to further the home to school connection.

SKU: 1008

$1.00

Word Family Books - ank | This word family booklet emphasizes the word family — ank. It goes great in a station or as individual work sent home to further the home to school connection.

SKU: 1015

$1.00

Word Family Books - ar | This word family booklet emphasizes the word family — ar. It goes great in a station or as individual work sent home to further the home to school connection.

SKU: 1017

$1.00

Word Family Books - ash | This word family booklet emphasizes the word family — ash. It goes great in a station or as individual work sent home to further the home to school connection.

SKU: 1018

$1.00

Word Family Books - at | This word family booklet emphasizes the word family — at. It goes great in a station or as individual work sent home to further the home to school connection.

SKU: 1019

$1.00

Word Family Books - ate | This word family booklet emphasizes the word family — ate. It goes great in a station or as individual work sent home to further the home to school connection.

SKU: 1020

$1.00

Word Family Books - aw | This word family booklet emphasizes the word family — aw. It goes great in a station or as individual work sent home to further the home to school connection.

SKU: 1021

$1.00

Word Family Books - eat | This word family booklet emphasizes the word family — eat. It goes great in a station or as individual work sent home to further the home to school connection.

SKU: 1022

$1.00

Word Family Books - eel | This word family booklet emphasizes the word family — eel. It goes great in a station or as individual work sent home to further the home to school connection.

SKU: 1023

$1.00

Word Family Books - eet | This word family booklet emphasizes the word family — eet. It goes great in a station or as individual work sent home to further the home to school connection.

SKU: 1025

$1.00

Word Family Books - ell | This word family booklet emphasizes the word family — ell. It goes great in a station or as individual work sent home to further the home to school connection.

SKU: 1026

$1.00

Word Family Books - en | This word family booklet emphasizes the word family — en. It goes great in a station or as individual work sent home to further the home to school connection.

SKU: 1028

$1.00

Word Family Books - ent | This word family booklet emphasizes the word family – ent. It goes great in a station or as individual work sent home to further the home to school connection.

SKU: 1029

$1.00

Word Family Books - est | This word family booklet emphasizes the word family – est. It goes great in a station or as individual work sent home to further the home to school connection.

SKU: 1027

$1.00

Word Family Books - ice | This word family booklet emphasizes the word family – ice. It goes great in a station or as individual work sent home to further the home to school connection.

SKU: 1030

$1.00

Word Family Books - ick | This word family booklet emphasizes the word family – ick. It goes great in a station or as individual work sent home to further the home to school connection.

SKU: 1031

$1.00

Word Family Books - ide | This word family booklet emphasizes the word family – ide. It goes great in a station or as individual work sent home to further the home to school connection.

SKU: 1032

$1.00

Word Family Books - ife | This word family booklet emphasizes the word family – ife. It goes great in a station or as individual work sent home to further the home to school connection.

SKU: 1033

$1.00

Word Family Books - ight | This word family booklet emphasizes the word family – ight. It goes great in a station or as individual work sent home to further the home to school connection.

SKU: 1034

$1.00

Word Family Books - ile | This word family booklet emphasizes the word family – ile. It goes great in a station or as individual work sent home to further the home to school connection.

SKU: 1035

$1.00

Word Family Books - ill | This word family booklet emphasizes the word family – ill. It goes great in a station or as individual work sent home to further the home to school connection.

SKU: 1036

$1.00

Word Family Books - in | This word family booklet emphasizes the word family — in. It goes great in a station or as individual work sent home to further the home to school connection.

SKU: 1040

$1.00

Word Family Books - ing | This word family booklet emphasizes the word family — ing. It goes great in a station or as individual work sent home to further the home to school connection.

SKU: 1038

$1.00

Word Family Books - ink | This word family booklet emphasizes the word family — ink. It goes great in a station or as individual work sent home to further the home to school connection.

SKU: 1039

$1.00

Word Family Books - ip | This word family booklet emphasizes the word family — ip. It goes great in a station or as individual work sent home to further the home to school connection.

SKU: 1041

$1.00

Word Family Books - it | This word family booklet emphasizes the word family — it. It goes great in a station or as individual work sent home to further the home to school connection.

SKU: 1042

$1.00

Word Family Books - oak | This word family booklet emphasizes the word family — oak. It goes great in a station or as individual work sent home to further the home to school connection.

SKU: 1043

$1.00

Word Family Books - ock | This word family booklet emphasizes the word family — ock. It goes great in a station or as individual work sent home to further the home to school connection.

SKU: 1044

$1.00

Word Family Books - oil | This word family booklet emphasizes the word family — oil. It goes great in a station or as individual work sent home to further the home to school connection.

SKU: 1048

$1.00

Word Family Books - on | This word family booklet emphasizes the word family — on. It goes great in a station or as individual work sent home to further the home to school connection.

SKU: 1061

$1.00

Word Family Books - one | This word family booklet emphasizes the word family — one. It goes great in a station or as individual work sent home to further the home to school connection.

SKU: 1037

$1.00

Word Family Books - oo | This word family booklet emphasizes the word family — oo. It goes great in a station or as individual work sent home to further the home to school connection.

SKU: 1056

$1.00

Word Family Books - ood (as in Good) | This word family booklet emphasizes the word family — ood (as in Good). It goes great in a station or as individual work sent home to further the home to school connection.

SKU: 1045

$1.00

Word Family Books - ood (as in Mood) | This word family booklet emphasizes the word family — ood (as in Mood). It goes great in a station or as individual work sent home to further the home to school connection.

SKU: 1047

$1.00

Word Family Books - oof | This word family booklet emphasizes the word family — oof. It goes great in a station or as individual work sent home to further the home to school connection.

SKU: 1057

$1.00

Word Family Books - ook | This word family booklet emphasizes the word family — ook. It goes great in a station or as individual work sent home to further the home to school connection.

SKU: 1058

$1.00

Word Family Books - oom | This word family booklet emphasizes the word family — oom. It goes great in a station or as individual work sent home to further the home to school connection.

SKU: 1059

$1.00

Word Family Books - op | This word family booklet emphasizes the word family — op. It goes great in a station or as individual work sent home to further the home to school connection.

SKU: 1062

$1.00

Word Family Books - ore | This word family booklet emphasizes the word family — ore. It goes great in a station or as individual work sent home to further the home to school connection.

SKU: 1063

$1.00

Word Family Books - orn | This word family booklet emphasizes the word family — orn. It goes great in a station or as individual work sent home to further the home to school connection.

SKU: 1064

$1.00

Word Family Books - ot | This word family booklet emphasizes the word family — ot. It goes great in a station or as individual work sent home to further the home to school connection.

SKU: 1065

$1.00

Word Family Books - ought | This word family booklet emphasizes the word family — ought. It goes great in a station or as individual work sent home to further the home to school connection.

SKU: 1066

$1.00

Word Family Books - ould | This word family booklet emphasizes the word family — ould. It goes great in a station or as individual work sent home to further the home to school connection.

SKU: 1067

$1.00

Word Family Books - ouse | This word family booklet emphasizes the word family — ouse. It goes great in a station or as individual work sent home to further the home to school connection.

SKU: 1068

$1.00

Word Family Books - out | This word family booklet emphasizes the word family — out. It goes great in a station or as individual work sent home to further the home to school connection.

SKU: 1069

$1.00

Word Family Books - ow (as in Snow) | This word family booklet emphasizes the word family — ow (as in Snow). It goes great in a station or as individual work sent home to further the home to school connection.

SKU: 1046

$1.00

Word Family Books - ow (like cow) | This word family booklet emphasizes the word family — ow (like cow). It goes great in a station or as individual work sent home to further the home to school connection.

SKU: 1070

$1.00

Word Family Books - own | This word family booklet emphasizes the word family — own. It goes great in a station or as individual work sent home to further the home to school connection.

SKU: 1071

$1.00

Word Family Books - uck | This word family booklet emphasizes the word family – uck. It goes great in a station or as individual work sent home to further the home to school connection.

SKU: 1072

$1.00

Word Family Books - ug | This word family booklet emphasizes the word family – ug. It goes great in a station or as individual work sent home to further the home to school connection.

SKU: 1073

$1.00

Word Family Books - ump | This word family booklet emphasizes the word family – ump. It goes great in a station or as individual work sent home to further the home to school connection.

SKU: 1074

$1.00

Word Family Books - un | This word family booklet emphasizes the word family – un. It goes great in a station or as individual work sent home to further the home to school connection.

SKU: 1075

$1.00

Word Family Books - unk | This word family booklet emphasizes the word family – unk. It goes great in a station or as individual work sent home to further the home to school connection.

SKU: 1076

$1.00

World Family Book - all | This word family booklet emphasizes the word family - all. It goes great in a station or as individual work sent home to further the home to school connection.

SKU: 1006

$1.00

WRITING

	7 Steps to a Constructed Response	These 7 steps will give them the confidence they need as writers. They will learn the 7 steps and attach a visual image to each one to help them remember the writing process. SKU: 3063	$3.00
	**I - Write Foldable	SPANISH**	This item contains a three-part foldable to create a movable I-Write Plan. The foldable is adjustable based on how much textual evidence a student would like to use. SKU: 3078	$5.00
	I-Write Foldable	This item contains a three-part foldable to create a movable I-Write Plan. The foldable is adjustable based on how much textual evidence a student would like to use. SKU: 1000	$5.00
	I-Write Plan - Poster Set	The I-Write Plan Posters Set - Students learn best when all of the learning styles are addressed. This activity allows for verbal, visual, and kinesthetic involvement while learning the parts of a short constructed response. SKU: 2037	$5.00
	Prompt to Product - Interactive ECR SKU: 6067	$20.00
	Question Stem Synonym Booklets SKU: 3053	$8.00
	Research Briefs SKU: 9038	$12.00
	Thesis Human Matching Squares SKU: 4040	$7.00

	TRACKS	The parts of a passage and the secrets of a source	$2.00
	SKU: 4030	
	What Happens When?	$12.00
	SKU: 9039	

Teach Big
Full Circle Language Arts
Teacher Resources

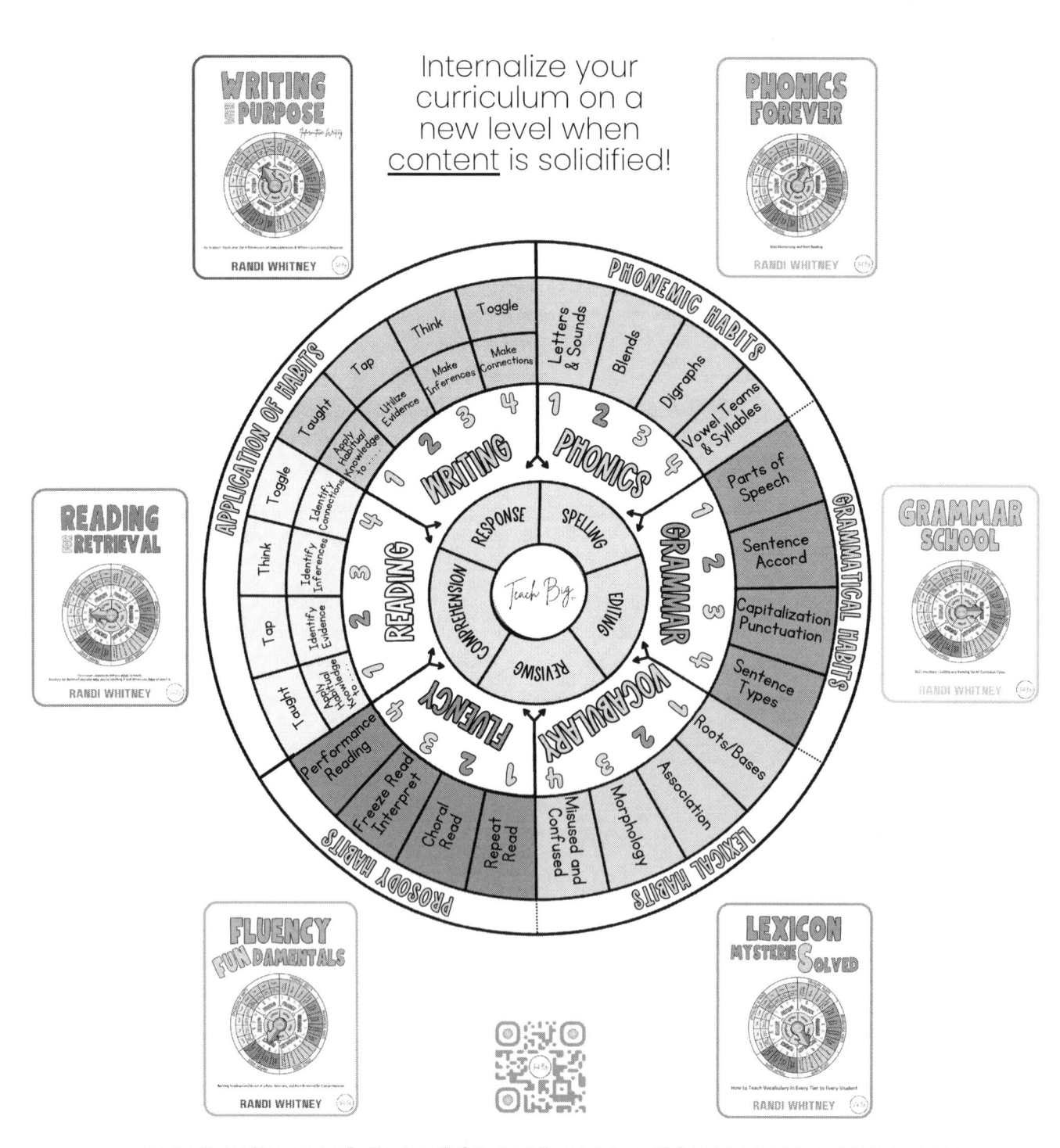

Internalize your curriculum on a new level when **content** is solidified!

AN EXTENSIVE ELAR RESOURCE SYSTEM TO SUPPORT YOUR CURRICULUM

TEACHBIG.COM   2025 Copyright Teach BIG Reading and Writing   281-549-4466

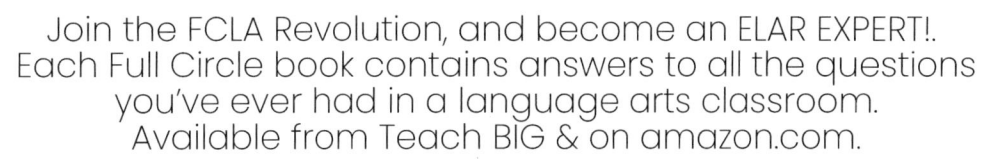

FULL CIRCLE LANGUAGE ARTS SERIES DESCRIPTIONS

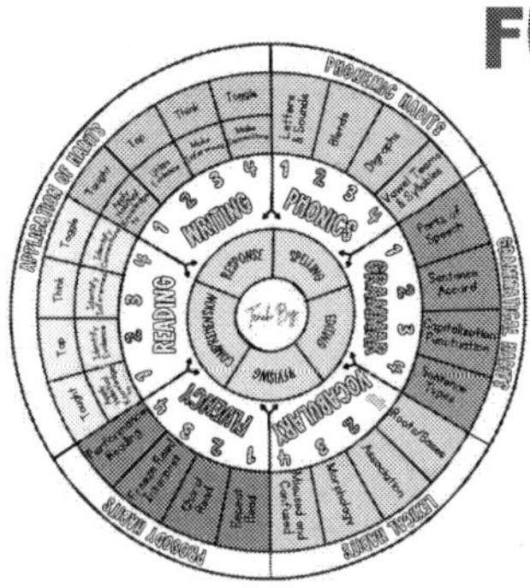

Join the FCLA Revolution, and become an ELAR EXPERT!. Each Full Circle book contains answers to all the questions you've ever had in a language arts classroom. Available from Teach BIG & on amazon.com.

Visit our website to see the corresponding teacher trainings and student camps!

teachbig.com

Phonics Forever is more than just a book—it's a comprehensive guide to teaching phonics in a way that is purposeful, powerful, and permanently embedded in students' learning.

Rooted in the core principles of the Science of Reading, this resource moves beyond surface-level phonics drills and dive deep into the four quadrants of phonics instruction—ensuring that students build lasting, transferable skills in decoding, encoding, fluency, and word knowledge, including:

- Explicit guidance on aligning phonics instruction to the Science of Reading, ensuring every lesson supports cognitive load, structured literacy, and comprehension.
- Strategies for embedding phonics into all areas of reading and writing, including whole group, small group, and independent literacy time.
- Tools for connecting phonics to vocabulary, fluency, and grammar.
- Engaging classroom activities, routines, and games that reinforce phonics skills in meaningful ways.
- Support for differentiating phonics instruction to meet the needs of all learners.

498 PAGES

Grammar School is your ultimate classroom companion—a powerhouse resource filled with everything you need to transform the way your students approach grammar, editing, and revising. Designed for teachers who want practical tools that fit seamlessly into any curriculum, this book equips you with fresh strategies, actionable ideas, and engaging activities that will make your grammar instruction unforgettable.

Here's what you'll find inside *Grammar School*:

- Lesson Plans that break down complex concepts into easy-to-teach steps.
- Teacher Training Scripts to help you introduce key ideas with confidence and clarity.
- Poems, Songs, and Chants that make tricky grammar rules stick.
- Reader's Theater Dramas to engage students and bring grammar to life.
- Thousands of Mentor Sentences and Examples to use as teaching tools.
- Mock Assessment Questions with Answer Choices to build test-taking skills.
- Intervention Activities that stop confusion in its tracks and help every student succeed.

480 PAGES

Unlock the power of words in your classroom with *Lexicon Mysteries Solved*, the ultimate guide for teachers seeking to transform vocabulary instruction into a meaningful and engaging experience. Packed with actionable activities, creative lesson plans, and real-world examples, this book equips you with everything you need to empower your students to decode, analyze, and confidently use new words.

Discover practical tools to teach within *Lexicon Mysteries Solved*:

- Word Origins and Morphology: Break down and understand complex words
- Collocations, Word Associations, and Context Clues: Build strong foundational skills
- Poetry, Drama, & Literary Terms: Make literature come alive with clear explanations and dynamic activities
- Tiered Vocabulary, Academic Vocabulary, and Word Consciousness: Differentiate instruction to meet the needs of every learner

Engage your students with interactive activities like scavenger hunts, group storytelling, and role-playing.

349 PAGES

Fluency Fundamentals is the ultimate resource for your biggest questions about reading fluency.

Inside, you'll find research-based answers to the most common fluency questions:
- What is fluency, and why does it matter for reading success?
- How can I effectively assess fluency to guide instruction?
- What are the best ways to help students improve fluency?
- How do I support students who read accurately but too slowly?
- What can I do for students who read too quickly and without expression?
- How do I build fluency in students with decoding difficulties?
- What strategies keep fluency practice engaging and fun?
- How does fluency connect to comprehension, and how can I ensure understanding?
- How can I differentiate fluency instruction for diverse learners?
- How much time should I dedicate to fluency instruction?

308 PAGES

Reading for Retrieval is an essential companion every language arts teacher needs!

- Discover every aspect of every literary element, and explore how the state constructs reading comprehension questions and answer choices regarding each literary element
- Utilize activities, conversation starters, acronyms for quick recall, real-world examples, mentor texts, and assessment questions that span all levels of language comprehension
- Master the nuances of author's purpose and theme
- Explore complex inferencing skills and the layers of textual evidence
- Learn the "how" and the "why" of teaching the 4 Dimensions of Reading

Reading for Retrieval guides and transforms - whether you are a veteran teacher or you are new to education! Regardless of the curriculum, the standards, or the grade level, this book is a timeless resource for those who want students to grasp language arts at the highest level for their potentials.

470 PAGES

Writing with Purpose is a practical, step-by-step guide to teaching writing in a way that is both engaging and effective. This book breaks down the entire writing process, from analyzing prompts and crafting thesis statements to using textual evidence with confidence and writing with a clear purpose.

Inside *Writing with Purpose*, You Will Find:
- A structured approach to breaking down writing into manageable, teachable steps
- Engaging, hands-on activities that get students thinking critically and writing purposefully
- Mentor text sets that show students how to analyze strong writing and apply quality techniques
- Practical tools for teaching constructed responses, from shaping prompts to citing evidence
- Classroom-ready lesson plans and activities that help teachers implement purpose-driven writing instruction immediately for SCR and ECR responses
- Encouragement and motivation to help teachers overcome frustration and inspire students to love writing....Yes! That's really possible!

468 PAGES

The WRITE to Argue is more than just a book—it's a complete resource for teaching students how to argue with purpose, precision, and confidence.

With *The WRITE to Argue*, teachers receive a treasure trove of resources, including:
- Step-by-step guide for argumentative writing, from shaping a prompt to crafting conclusions
- Guidance for writing effective claims and building strong, evidence-based arguments
- A deep dive into ethos, pathos, and logos, helping students persuade with logic, emotion, and credibility
- The CSI Approach to textual evidence, turning students into detectives who cite relevant evidence
- Strategies for constructing counterarguments and rebuttals that strengthen students' writing
- Sentence starters and tips for smooth transitions, keeping writing clear and cohesive
- Ready-to-use templates and activities for immediate classroom implementation

300 PAGES

TEACH BIG STUDENT MATERIALS

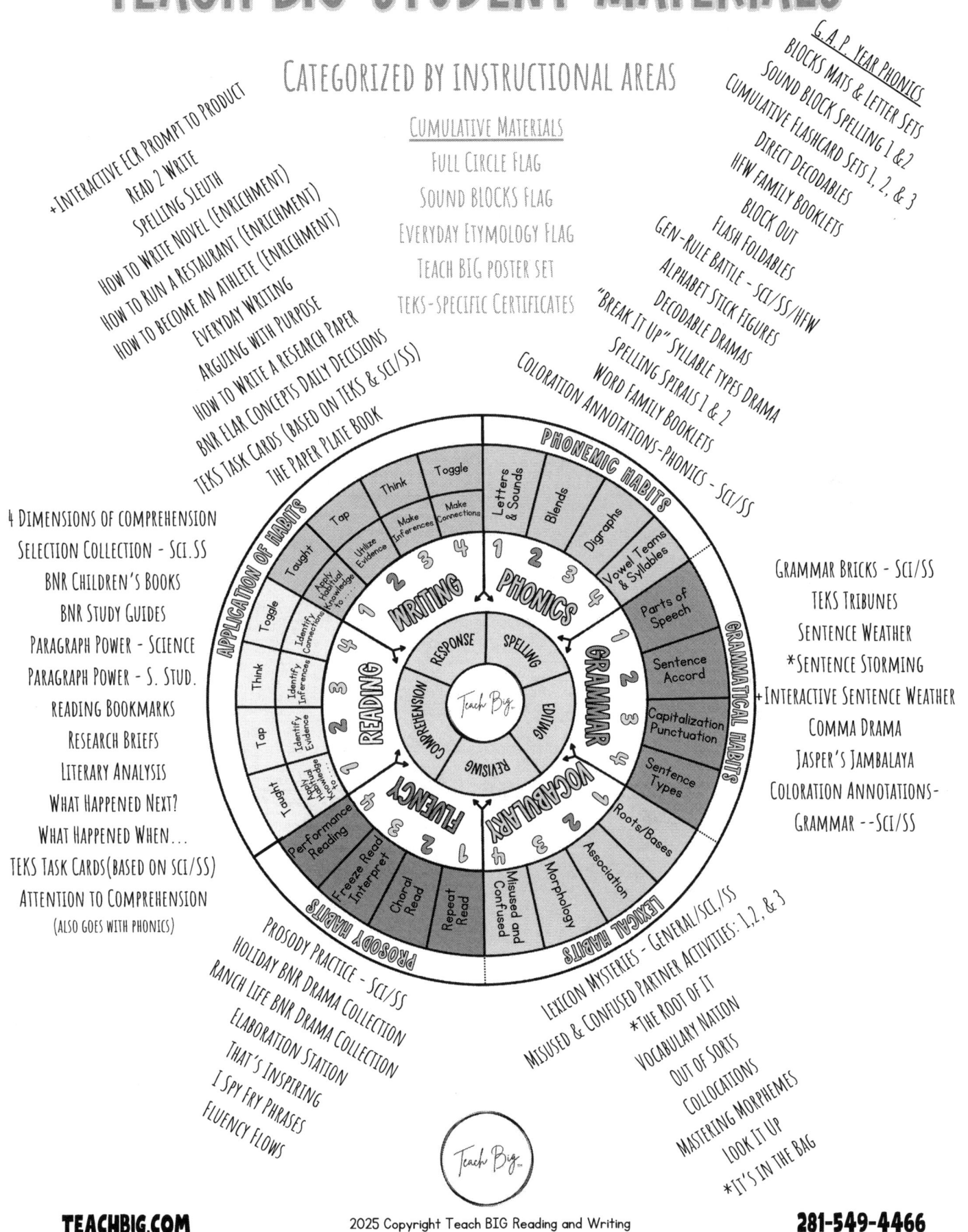

Categorized by Instructional Areas

Cumulative Materials
- Full Circle Flag
- Sound BLOCKS Flag
- Everyday Etymology Flag
- Teach BIG Poster Set
- TEKS-Specific Certificates

Writing / Application of Habits
- +Interactive ECR Prompt to Product
- Read 2 Write
- Spelling Sleuth
- How to Write Novel (Enrichment)
- How to Run a Restaurant (Enrichment)
- How to Become an Athlete (Enrichment)
- Everyday Writing
- Arguing with Purpose
- How to Write a Research Paper
- BNR ELAR Concepts Daily Decisions
- TEKS Task Cards (based on TEKS & Sci/SS)
- The Paper Plate Book

Reading / Comprehension
- 4 Dimensions of Comprehension
- Selection Collection – Sci.SS
- BNR Children's Books
- BNR Study Guides
- Paragraph Power – Science
- Paragraph Power – S. Stud.
- Reading Bookmarks
- Research Briefs
- Literary Analysis
- What Happened Next?
- What Happened When…
- TEKS Task Cards (based on Sci/SS)
- Attention to Comprehension
  (also goes with phonics)

Phonics / Phonemic Habits
- G.A.P. Year Phonics
- Blocks Mats & Letter Sets
- Sound Block Spelling 1 & 2
- Cumulative Flashcard Sets 1, 2, & 3
- Direct Decodables
- HFW Family Booklets
- Block Out
- Flash Foldables
- Gen-Rule Battle – Sci/SS/HFW
- Alphabet Stick Figures
- Decodable Dramas
- "Break It Up" Syllable Types Drama
- Spelling Spirals 1 & 2
- Word Family Booklets
- Coloration Annotations – Phonics – Sci/SS

Grammar / Grammatical Habits
- Grammar Bricks – Sci/SS
- TEKS Tribunes
- Sentence Weather
- *Sentence Storming
- +Interactive Sentence Weather
- Comma Drama
- Jasper's Jambalaya
- Coloration Annotations – Grammar – Sci/SS

Vocabulary / Lexical Habits
- Lexicon Mysteries – General/Sci/SS
- Misused & Confused Partner Activities: 1, 2, & 3
- *The Root of It
- Vocabulary Nation
- Out of Sorts
- Collocations
- Mastering Morphemes
- Look It Up
- *It's in the Bag

Fluency / Prosody Habits
- Prosody Practice – Sci/SS
- Holiday BNR Drama Collection
- Ranch Life BNR Drama Collection
- Elaboration Station
- That's Inspiring
- I Spy Fry Phrases
- Fluency Flows

TEACHBIG.COM 2025 Copyright Teach BIG Reading and Writing **281-549-4466**

Teach Big

Order date:

_____ / _____ / _____

Use this form to order products and from the Teach BIG Catalog

Visit teachbig.com to place an order online.
Contact us at welcome@teachbig.com regarding services

CUSTOMER INFORMATION:

Name: _____

Phone: _____

Email: _____

Purchase Order # _____

Address: _____

City: _____ State: _____ Zip: _____

School/District: _____

ORDER DETAILS:

ITEM SKU	DESCRIPTION	QTY	PRICE	AMOUNT

SUBTOTAL	
SHIPPING (15%)	
TAX (8.25%)	
TOTAL	

☐ Purchase Order Enclosed

☐ Check Enclosed (Payable to Teach BIG)

☐ Request Invoice

☐ Pay Online at teachbig.com

THANK YOU FOR YOUR ORDER & WELCOME TO THE TEACH BIG COMMUNITY!

Made in the USA
Columbia, SC
26 May 2025